THERAPEUTIC
JOURNAL
WRITING

Writing for Therapy or Personal Development Series
Edited by Gillie Bolton

Writing for Therapy or Personal Development, a foundation library to a rapidly developing field, covers the theory and practice of key areas. Clearly exemplified, engaging and accessible, the series is appropriate for therapeutic, healthcare, or creative writing practitioners and facilitators, and for individual writers or courses.

other books in the series

Writing Routes
A Resource Handbook of Therapeutic Writing
Edited by Gillie Bolton, Victoria Janet Field and Kate Thompson
Foreword by Gwyneth Lewis
ISBN 978 1 84905 107 1

Writing Works
A Resource Handbook for Therapeutic Writing Workshops and Activities
Edited by Gillie Bolton, Victoria Field and Kate Thompson
Foreword by Blake Morrison
ISBN 978 1 84310 468 1

Write Yourself
Creative Writing and Personal Development
Gillie Bolton
ISBN 978 1 84905 110 1

Poetry and Story Therapy
The Healing Power of Creative Expression
Geri Giebel Chavis
ISBN 978 1 84905 832 2

Writing in Bereavement
A Creative Handbook
Jane Moss
ISBN 978 1 84905 212 2

THERAPEUTIC JOURNAL WRITING

An Introduction for Professionals

Kate Thompson

Foreword by Kathleen Adams

Jessica Kingsley *Publishers*
London and Philadelphia

First published in 2011
by Jessica Kingsley Publishers
116 Pentonville Road
London N1 9JB, UK
and
400 Market Street, Suite 400
Philadelphia, PA 19106, USA

www.jkp.com

Copyright © Kate Thompson 2011
Foreword copyright © Kathleen Adams 2011
Printed digitally since 2012

Library of Congress Cataloging in Publication Data
Thompson, Kate, 1961-
  Therapeutic journal writing : an introduction for professionals
/ Kate Thompson ; foreword by Kathleen Adams.
      p. ; cm.
  Includes bibliographical references and index.
  ISBN 978-1-84310-690-6 (alk. paper)
  1. Diaries--Therapeutic use. I. Title.
  [DNLM: 1. Writing. 2. Counseling--methods. 3. Psychotherapy-
-methods. WM 450.5.W9 T473t 2010]
  RC489.D5T52 2010
  616.89'165--dc22
                              2010019749

British Library Cataloguing in Publication Data
A CIP catalogue record for this book is available from the British Library

ISBN 978 1 84310 690 6

Acknowledgements

I want to thank my own clients, supervisees and students who have told me their stories, particularly S who is wiser than she knows and is an example to all of us who use journals for healing and growth. I also thank all my colleagues in the Lapidus and the Center for Journal Therapy communities for their support and encouragement throughout this process and to Gillie Bolton, Emmy van Deurzen and of course Kay Adams for being my wise mentors, supervisors and friends. Also, to my editor at JKP, Stephen Jones.

Contents

Foreword

In the opening months of the twenty-first century I penned this three-line journal entry:

> Kate T. from London came to writing group this afternoon.
> She is lovely. I hope we will do some work together. Perhaps
> become friends?

In the ensuing decade, I have been privileged first to serve as Kate Thompson's mentor in the fast-growing field of journal therapy, and then as a colleague and friend on both sides of the Atlantic. I have also borne witness as she has emerged as the preeminent journal therapist in the UK, both from the provider standpoint and also in her work as a Board-certified supervisor of other therapists.

Kate's book draws equally from both areas of her expertise. In her role as facilitator of the emerging voices of new journal keepers, she cogently recaps the prevailing wisdom in the field and adds her own interpretations. Writing techniques learned from the pioneers spring to vibrant, three-dimensional life through her personal stories and the illustrative examples of her clients. Each weaves in perceptive writing prompts, making the reach for one's own journal nearly irresistible.

Equally deft is her clinician's voice as she brings practical guidance to those seeking to offer therapeutic journal writing in a professional practice context. Informed by her years of experience as a Certified Journal to the

Self® Instructor and a credentialed psychotherapist and supervisor, Kate lays out a road map for facilitators. She marks the ground for therapeutic writing groups, notes writing interventions and strategies for common clinical disorders, and outlines a superb plan for using journal writing in supervision of all types: individual, group, peer and self-supervision.

In the past, there has been a dearth of clinical theory and application in the therapeutic writing literature, and this book contributes to our understanding of the potential applications for therapeutic journal writing. Since 2006, I have travelled the United States teaching approximately 4500 American psychotherapists my core theories in journal therapy. I begin each workshop by asking participants to write an ending to this sentence stem: 'When my patients and clients write journals…' Then, when I return from my travels, I tally the responses and enter the results into a spreadsheet. The top answers, in order, are as follows:

1. As a result of writing journals, the clients/patients develop insight, clarity, awareness about their lives, behaviours, problems, families and personal histories.

2. Feelings are more readily expressed and released. Catharsis happens. Patients and clients learn about identification, regulation and expression of emotions.

3. Clients and patients struggle. They founder in the absence of informed guidance about therapeutic journal writing. They resist, they refuse, they start and quickly stop.

4. Therapy moves faster when a program of therapeutic journal writing is undertaken, because the therapy hour can be extended into the space and time between sessions, with the clients/patients taking responsibility for their own self-exploration.

It is clear that journal therapy is both a natural fit and an urgently needed tool to address four therapeutic tasks of any counselling situation: the development of insight; the recognition and appropriate expression of emotions; the engagement in the healing process; and the self-reliance to resolve one's own problems. In this remarkable book, Kate Thompson has expertly addressed these tasks by offering both consumers/clients and facilitators/therapists clear, steady guidance for the journal journey.

Kathleen Adams LPC
Director, Center for Journal Therapy, Denver CO USA
Author, Journal to the Self *and* The Way of the Journal

Preface

Who is this book for?

This book is one that I would have welcomed at various stages in my life, particularly as I went on my professional journey. I have used therapeutic journal writing for my own healing and growth (first cathartically like many adolescents and later as a more reflective practice – see *Afterword*). This book would have helped me to use it more consciously and given me a structure and a set of techniques to use.

My intention is that this book will be useful to practitioners in the 'people professions'. I hope that practitioners including counsellors, social workers, mental health workers, nurses, life coaches, health professionals, teachers, lecturers, and writing facilitators of all kinds, will find a place for therapeutic journal writing, within their work with others.

To reflect the range of practitioners whom I hope will find this book a useful resource, I include the experiences and opinions of a range of individuals, operating in different practice settings, who attended my training sessions.

Although many of the examples are drawn from therapeutic situations, it is my intention that these are examples only, and that they may also be taken as applicable to other settings. Similarly, where mention is made, for simplicity's sake, of 'client' or 'clients' this could equally be applied to service users, students or group members. Finally, there is no gender bias in this work and the female pronoun should be seen as inclusive.

When I became a counsellor I naturally wanted to share journal writing as a therapeutic practice in my work with clients (after all it had worked for me) but I wasn't sure it was OK to do so (Thompson and Wright 2006). This book would have reassured me that it was. I would have seen that incorporating therapeutic journal writing into my counselling work was a legitimate practice (that is, the use of journal writing as an adjunct to counselling (Thompson 2004) to support the tasks of therapy within a talking relationship was something that others had done before). Furthermore this book would have deepened my understanding and provided examples of different cases and techniques which I could then have confidently employed.

The next stage in my professional life was to develop a supervision practice and to become a British Association for Counselling and Psychotherapy (BACP) senior accredited supervisor. This book would have shown me applications of therapeutic journal writing within that context and that would have shown me the logical next step.

Then I discovered that there was, in the US, the Center for Journal Therapy. My first reaction was, 'Of course' and then, 'why didn't I know about this?' I naturally trained there as a journal therapist.

So at each stage of my professional journey I have used therapeutic journal writing with clients, supervisees and with myself to monitor my own process both in my professional practice and in my life. I hope that others will be able to do the same and will take from this book the ideas and practices I have discovered and make them their own.

So, what is therapeutic journal writing?

> Journal therapy – the purposeful and intentional use of reflective writing to further mental, physical, emotional and spiritual health and wellness – is an effective means of providing focus and clarity to issues, concerns, conflicts and confusions. (The Center for Journal Therapy 2004)

The definition above was written to describe a particular form of therapeutic journal writing, journal therapy, but effectively describes the core purpose and function of therapeutic journal writing. In addition, therapeutic journal writing comprises a set of techniques which can be adopted and integrated into other forms of therapy, unlike journal therapy, which is a standalone modality like music therapy, drama therapy or art therapy.

Some clients choose therapeutic journal writing because they want to write rather than talk; others come upon it almost by chance, perhaps introduced to the techniques by their therapist within the context of other therapeutic intervention or by discovering the therapeutic potential of their own journals and seeking to develop this.

Therapeutic journal writing can be embedded within the professional practice of many different kinds of practitioner – both for themselves and for their students, clients, supervisees and patients to encourage healing and wellbeing. This book aims to provide enough information about techniques, structures and applications to make therapeutic journal writing accessible to people in all branches of the helping professions, for them to use it with others and as a professional support for themselves. If practitioners find it of personal benefit too then that is a bonus.

Defining therapeutic journal writing

I begin with the premise that journal writing is both a creative and a therapeutic act. Journal writing is broader than many people think. As we will see, it encompasses many writing activities that may not have previously been considered to be journal writing; it is not necessarily a daily written record of activity.

Journal writing may therefore be therapeutic and include any personal writing which brings another insight or perspective on our lives. However, therapeutic journal writing implies the conscious intent and deliberate attempt to write in ways which will produce change, healing and growth. Therapeutic journal writing takes particular writing techniques and uses them to support the tasks of therapy. It is a reflective (thinking about, pondering, exploring) and a reflexive (integrating and using the awareness gained from reflecting) practice which can help to develop greater understanding of self and the world and self-in-the world, offering a way of looking at the self, relationships and context in writing.

People who consciously engage in therapeutic journal writing, often report that they experience greater wellbeing, understanding and insight into themselves as a result of the practice. They say that their lives are enriched and they feel they live more fully. Other more concrete benefits can include problem resolution, clarity in decision-making, relationship healing, improved time-management and project planning.

In addition to being a therapeutic act, journal writing is also a creative act. Readers like creative writing group facilitator Jane, who attended one of my training sessions, may be educationalists and writers rather than therapists. They may be creative writers themselves or work with creative writers. They will find the techniques and exercises in this book allow for fresh ways of expressing their creativity or, in particular, working through writers' blocks.

Any personal development increases a writer's self-knowledge and has an effect on what they produce. However, it should be acknowledged that journal writing is part of the journey rather than the destination. In other words, therapeutic journal writing is definitely 'process' writing not 'product' (these terms are explained on pp.28–9): reflection, not editing, is the second stage in this type of writing and the intention is not to create a finished or publishable piece of work.

As a BACP senior accredited counsellor and supervisor I work from an existential perspective. This means that I am interested in the way individuals relate to their worlds and see my role as helping them to understand and clarify their worldview and their experiences.

> Existential thinking is a steadfast and loyal endeavour to reflect on everyday human in order to make sense of it. As a practice it is probably as old as the human reality ability to reflect. (Van Deurzen 2009, p.1)

> Existential psychotherapy does not seek to cure or explain, it merely seeks to explore, describe and clarify in order to try to understand the human predicament. (Van Deurzen 2009, p.4)

In the context of this work I have come across many people for whom journal writing can offer an additional way of looking at the self and finding another way through the difficulties of their lives and their existential concerns. Ultimately the most important relationship is the relationship with the self, and journal writing can develop the intimacy with the self which allows other relationships to flourish.

> The way in which I tell my story is the way in which I create a self… Our stories change as we live and so we are changed too. (Van Deurzen 2008)

Using therapeutic journal writing in practice

Therapeutic journal writing can become a part of professional practice for people working in both clinical settings (such as primary care counsellors or psychiatric nurses) and non-clinical settings (such as social workers or creative writing facilitators). It can be used with clients, students or supervisees and can be integrated to provide support for the practitioner in supervision or self-supervision. The reader might:

- work clinically with others and want to introduce or expand their use of writing as a therapeutic medium either as part of another form of treatment or activity (journal writing as an adjunct to other therapeutic interventions) or as a therapeutic activity in its own right; or

- use journal writing with others in non-clinical settings (for example in education or in community settings) and wish to develop a new approach and discover new techniques.

The reader might be someone who wants to use journal writing for themselves in their professional lives, either:

- as a practical tool in the pursuit of their professional duties, such as for organization, planning or time management; or

- as a means of self-supervision within their practice either clinically or developmentally.

The professional and the personal areas of our experience often overlap. We do not (and indeed cannot, whether we wish to or not) leave our professional selves at the door on the way in or out of the classroom, clinic or therapy room. Therapeutic journal writing can help to manage transitions and movements between different spheres of activity and integrate different areas of our lives. In fact, many of the techniques in this book can be applied in both professional and personal ways for ourselves or with others.

Some readers may use therapeutic journal writing for personal development – such readers will find lots of ideas for how to use techniques for particular situations. This book goes through various stages from getting started to going deeper. There are lots of case examples of how other people have used the ideas for further inspiration. This approach is for anyone who wants to use therapeutic journal writing as a means of self-directed change, healing and growth.

Structure of the book

You can initially choose to read the book from beginning to end or to dip into the parts which seem most relevant to you. At the end of each chapter, I include journal prompts to get you started on your way to understanding and using therapeutic journal writing.

Part One, 'Understanding the Basics' covers the principles involved in therapeutic journal writing – what it is, how it works and how it can be incorporated into practice.

It starts with an introduction which covers the background, history and key concepts in therapeutic journal writing.

Then, Chapter 1 deals with the practicalities: whether you are introducing therapeutic journal writing with others or starting to use it yourself, you first need to choose materials and decide how or where you want to write.

Chapter 2 explores how to incorporate therapeutic journal writing into professional practice, looking at different contexts, how to introduce it with others, working with groups, the role of the facilitator and client work.

Part Two describes the structured techniques that can be used. Each technique is explained in some detail in order to provide material for those who are introducing them to other people and those for whom they are unfamiliar. They are illustrated with case material from my journals and those of my students, colleagues, clients and supervisees.

Part Three goes on to describe less structured techniques, which become progressively more free.

The idea of progression from structured to freer techniques follows the principle defined in Kathleen Adams' Journal Ladder (1993, 1998), a developmental continuum of journal techniques designed to provide safety for vulnerable clients and to offer encouragement for less experienced practitioners.

Some techniques quickly go below the surface and allow insights and understanding to appear; some will even take us into the realm of the unconscious. There are times when this is the desired effect, others where it is more appropriate or useful to stay at a more concrete and known level.

Readers may choose to follow the development of techniques in these two parts from the most to the least structured; in this way it is possible to make a journey into an ever-deepening exploration of self and that self-in-the-world.

Once an understanding of therapeutic journal writing has been arrived at and the techniques experienced, you can incorporate the techniques into a structured repertoire of therapeutic journal writing. This can be used according to the reader's own judgement as to what is appropriate for different times and for different reasons.

Part Four provides further examples of how the techniques can be used in both clinical and non-clinical settings, including techniques that are particularly useful for using with different client groups and also the potential of therapeutic journal writing for supervision.

The ideas and examples in this part could be used by individuals working by themselves just as they can by therapists and other professionals with their clients, students or supervisees. If you are looking for a self-directed therapeutic intervention this part provides illustrations you can adapt to suit your own circumstances.

PART ONE

Understanding the Basics

Introduction

From journals to therapeutic journals

The first journals are thought to be cave paintings, 5500 years ago. These cave paintings may have told the story of a community, depicting its hunting, its homes and its people. Cave paintings also, it is thought, carried metaphorical and mythological meanings and developed layers of meaning and sophisticated narratives whose stories are still being unlocked.

The need to express history and tell stories of existence in whatever medium a society has available can be seen to be a highly primitive human urge. Journals are a way of finding the narrative, of depicting experience and relationships in people's lives. Narrative is a way of making sense of experience:

> In striving to make sense of life, persons face the task of arranging their experiences of events in sequences across time in such a way as to arrive at a coherent account of themselves and the world around them. (White and Epston 1990)

From evidence that archaeologists have uncovered, it seems narrative has always been part of human existence. In pre-literate societies drawing, painting, making things was a way of recording the stories. Constructing a narrative, or 'storying', is a highly therapeutic act for individuals or societies (White and Epston 1990; Etherington 2003; White 2007) and journal writing is one of the most available ways to engage in it today.

In more recent times, women would sew their stories in embroidery and quilts. As literacy developed in the upper and middle classes over the centuries, journals could be recorded through the written word. Women would typically write diaries of how to run an efficient house, making their experience visible or legible, but as their lives expanded so did the scope of their journals. The women who joined the Western settlers in the new world of the Americas were often isolated and they had to adapt to new ways of life (e.g. Snow 2000; Bird 1996). They kept individual journals in which they recorded their feelings and the rigours of their lives. These helped to ameliorate the loneliness and helped them to understand the lives being lived, so they were in a sense 'therapeutic' journals.

Men generally told larger stories in their journals and diaries because they appeared on a larger stage and would record their heroism, their adventures and their triumphs or defeats. Their journals were written to stand as monuments to their heroic masculinity.

Writing personal diaries and journals, the kind consisting of a mixture of description and reflection, or external observation and interior exploration, is an activity designed to increase understanding and insight for the writer. The move from descriptive journals to reflective and therefore inherently therapeutic journals began in the nineteenth century and went much further in the twentieth century. The development of therapeutic journal writing as an explicit and intentional form coincided with the growth of other therapeutic methods and activities throughout the twentieth century and continues today.

Then came books *about* writing journals; books which developed journal writing as a tool or methodology for growth and then as a therapeutic medium. These books started to appear in the twentieth century, and gave readers guidance and instruction on how to write journals. There are six groundbreaking authors who developed the field and best represent the move from the writing of journals and diaries as a way of recording individual lives to journal writing as a therapeutic medium. Their work spans the period from the 1930s to the end of the twentieth century:

1. **Marion Milner** was a pioneer of introspective journal writing as a way of examining her own thoughts and feelings. She originally published her work on this, *An Experiment in Leisure*, in the 1930s under the pseudonym Joanna Field; Virago re-published it in the 1980s under her own name. She used her journal writing as a method of understanding her own life and the nature of happiness (Milner 1986). After training as a psychoanalyst, much influenced by Jungian ideas, she used the technique as a form of supervision.

2. **Ira Progoff** was a New York psychologist who studied with Jung in Zurich and wrote the next book of the new genre. His work uses depth psychology and analytic ideas to inform his work with journal writing. *At a Journal Workshop* (Progoff 1975) describes The Intensive Journal™, a very particular method of keeping a journal for self-understanding and growth in which the writer or client creates sections for working with different techniques or time frames. Progoff developed this way of working in the 1960s to use with his clients as a therapeutic tool; initially he called the writings 'psychological notebooks'.

3. **Christina Baldwin** came from a humanist and feminist perspective and her work has embraced a spiritual dimension. She combines political consciousness with spiritual awareness through the medium of journal writing as self-actualization (to live to the fullest degree). *One to One* (Baldwin 1977) was her first book.

4. **Tristine Rainer** was inspired by diarist Anaïs Nin and looked at the techniques she employed. *The New Diary* (Rainer 1977) is a synthesis and development of diary writing techniques for personal growth. (Baldwin and Rainer were writing contemporaneously, but without knowledge of each other or the activity each was engaged in. They met when their first books were almost finished and Christina Baldwin now recalls thinking 'can there be room for two books on this very minority interest topic?').

5. **Kathleen Adams**, a psychotherapist working in Denver, Colorado, wrote *Journal to the Self: Twenty-two Paths to Personal Growth*

(Adams 1990) which is a guide for individuals. Her work offers a bridge from general journal writing to therapeutic journal writing techniques, which can be used in self-directed programmes or within the context of other therapeutic work. She also takes it further and develops programmes of Journal Therapy where the journal is the primary intentional modality rather than an adjunct to other forms of therapeutic work. Many of the techniques described in this book are adapted from her work.

6. **James Pennebaker**, a research psychologist in Austin, Texas, was the first person to conduct clinical trials on the health benefits of personal writing as a tool for healing and recovery and the physical effects of expressive writing. His work applies scientific method to analyse the effects of expressive writing on physical and psychological health. His many studies provide us with the most reliable data in this field. He has also developed a method of using expressive writing to heal trauma (Pennebaker 1990). His research looks at why and how writing works and documents the healing power of expressing emotion in language, in particular in written language. His work is fundamental in establishing a body of evidence to support what many of us know from our own experience.

Progoff, Milner, Baldwin, Rainer and Adams were all looking at how personal journal writing could be a tool to understand the self in greater detail and depth, how it could be used as a tool for healing and growth and how it could help us to understand the world of our own experience in order to make our lives, and those of our clients, students, supervisees, as rich and as fulfilling as possible. For these authors it was a conviction which arose from their own experience of the medium over long periods of time; their journals were a constant presence in their own lives.

As a research scientist Pennebaker's interest was rather different. Pennebaker is one of those who only keep a journal *in extremis* and in times of stress, but he has experienced personal benefit in doing so:

> In writing about upsetting events, for example, I often came to a new understanding of the emotional events themselves. Problems that had seemed overwhelming became more circumscribed and manageable after I saw them on paper. In

some way, writing about my haunting experiences helped
to resolve them. Once the issues were resolved, I no longer
thought about them. (Pennebaker 1990, p.89)

These authors are in no doubt about the therapeutic potential of journal
writing and they have amply demonstrated this for themselves and others.
Their work has established a strong tradition. Because of them, everyone
can benefit both professionally and personally from therapeutic journal
writing techniques tried and tested from the middle of the twentieth
century onwards.

This then was the beginning of therapeutic journal writing as a
particular form, as distinct from description or appointment keeping; it
marks the change from the unconscious therapeutic benefits of journal
keeping experienced by many journal-keepers over the centuries to
journal writing as an explicit therapeutic tool.

Diary or journal?

The word journal has its etymological roots in the French word *journée* –
a day. In the seventeenth century, *journée* also meant the distance travelled
in a day, a highly appropriate metaphor for the process we are talking
about here. It was also a record of the day's events (from which the term
'journalism' developed). Keeping a journal is a journey into the self and
with the self; it is also a record of the life lived.

Diary comes from the Latin *dies* (day) so also has that temporal sense
of a continuing existence, from day to day.

Although as an adolescent I felt I 'graduated' from 'diary' to 'journal',
the words are used interchangeably in this book. Of course people
constantly attempt to debate the differences and similarities between the
two and try to lay claim to the merit or distinction of one over the other
(this is rather like the debate between counselling and psychotherapy
– there's a rhythm to the argument whereby one area is claimed and
colonized by the champions of one term, only to find the champions
of the other are there as well). Some people believe that a diary is a
daily record of facts whereas a journal is a freer record of thoughts and
feelings.

An example of two books which support the interchangeability of
the words from a client perspective are Peter Woods' *Diary of a Grief*

(1998) and Christopher Rush's *To Travel Hopefully: Journal of a Death not Foretold* (2005). Both authors use writing to tell the story of their journeys through grief and ways of coping with the trauma of a spouse's death from cancer. Another two are by therapists: Jane Haynes' *Who is it That Can Tell Me Who I Am? The Journal of a Psychotherapist* (2007) and Marcia Hill's *Diary of a Country Therapist* (2004).

The etymological debate is further complicated by the usage in the UK of 'diary' to mean the place where all appointments, commitments and telephone numbers are recorded. In the US this would be a 'planner' or 'calendar'; in the UK the latter would be hung on the wall.

Product and process writing

In order to understand the nature of therapeutic journal writing, it is important from the outset to distinguish between 'product' and 'process' writing. Product writing is intended to produce a finished item, perhaps a poem, story or memoir. Process writing on the other hand is about the act of writing and recording itself.

Therapeutic journal writing in this context is definitely process writing. In its most basic sense this means that the outcome will not be measured by anyone other than the writer. Indeed, journal writing will often not be read or seen by anyone other than the writer and it will not be crafted or edited into a 'finished' piece, or product, at this stage. This may be permission enough for some people to begin journal writing, having freed their thoughts and feelings from potent and limiting earlier preconceptions about what writing 'should' be.

For some people, their journal entries will of course be the first step towards a product, such as a poem or story or article which in turn may or may not be published or shared. This idea of a journal being a 'first step' towards a product was used by a couple of the individuals mentioned at the start of this book:

Jane, a writer working in community settings who attended my classes, found that members of her groups or classes often wrote with this idea in mind, while Clare, a social worker, talked about some of her clients putting together an anthology about their lives as single mothers.

This kind of journal writing may be where the first thoughts and planning stages for a final piece occur. Many writers find that their notebooks or journals contain the seeds of subsequent creative activity and output (I would argue, though others would not agree, that a writer's notebook *is* a journal). Some people become published writers through the practice of journal writing. One of the benefits of journal writing can be the discovery of a creative voice, discovered when meeting the felicitous phrase or captivating description on the page. Reading the published journals of writers can be a journey through their creative development or the development of a published piece of work.

Christine Evans' book *Burning the Candle* (2006) consists of her long poem *Burning the Candle* and the journal which accompanied its writing. It is a fascinating insight into the creative process and the development of her relationship with herself and the poem as well as her reflections on her surroundings:

> Friday 2nd May 7 am
>
> My horse chestnut tree has no flowers, too young perhaps or not thriving where it's planted – is it growing towards them? Is a life of no account if it produces no flower, no seed, only grows and spreads arms out to the sky?
>
> This thought strikes with the force of an insight or a clue... (Evans 2006, p.71)
>
> All over again I am struck by how much we can call upon, stored below our every day thoughts. (Evans 2006, p.90)

However, for most people who practise therapeutic journal writing, the product of their process will be greater understanding, behavioural change or enhanced wellbeing rather than the writing itself.

Why therapeutic journal writing?

In the therapeutic journal writing classes I run, at the beginning of a new group I ask, 'Why are you here?'

The answers from a typical group are always something like this:

- 'To start keeping a journal'.
- 'To develop my creative writing'.

- 'To express myself and to focus'.
- 'To learn and to grow'.
- 'To explore myself and my experience'.
- 'To develop my journal writing and technique'.
- 'To find out who I am'.
- 'For self-discovery'.
- 'To do something for myself and find a pathway'.
- 'To relate to myself'.

When the group is for practitioners such as therapists on how to use therapeutic journal writing with their clients, the answers comprise many of the above but additionally include:

- 'To help my clients use a journal for therapeutic benefit'.
- 'To reflect on my work'.
- 'To learn more about therapeutic techniques'.

Some reasons for keeping a therapeutic journal

1. A journal is available at any time; it does not rely on the availability of other people or their willingness to listen or on someone's ability to pay for therapy.
   You can access your journal whenever you want at no cost.

2. Stories can be told and re-told *ad infinitum* in a journal. Repetition can be a valuable part of any healing process, but human listeners may get bored before the speaker does or before a point of change is reached.
   Your journal will never get bored with your words.

3. A journal provides a map of the journey towards growth, healing and change. Re-reading it gives a record of how and when change happens, a reminder that things do change and that change can happen gradually and almost imperceptibly and perhaps change can only be seen in retrospect.
   You can create your own therapeutic map.

4. A journal helps find a voice and to give voice to the previously unknown, unspeakable or unacknowledged. An authentic voice can first emerge in the journal.
    You can begin to hear your own voice.

5. A journal helps develop intimacy with the self. It allows different parts of the self to emerge and step forward from the unconscious (the familiar cry 'Where did that come from?' testifies to the power of this process).
    You can get to know yourself deeply.

6. A journal is a powerful organizational resource. It is a means of helping stay in control of life and develop coping strategies. It is invaluable as a time management tool for personal and professional activity.
    You can become better organized and able to cope.

7. A journal can be a rehearsal platform – for events, conversations, other writing, life itself and this helps to ameliorate anticipatory anxiety.
    You can practise for difficult or stressful experiences.

8. A journal validates experience – writing it down makes it real and confers existence on the writer. It makes the writer visible and will not judge what the writer says.
    You can begin to appear more substantial and solid in your journal.

9. A journal can contain uncomfortable states such as ambiguity or indecision and make them more bearable. In this way people can begin to mature.
    You can put all the unbearable bits of yourself in your journal and find they are bearable after all.

10. A journal is a way of developing and understanding a coherent narrative. It can repair a fractured life by giving shape to experience. When trauma causes a rupture in the narrative of a life keeping a therapeutic journal can restore it.
    You can repair the narrative of your life in your journal.

(adapted from Adams 1993, 1998)

Myths of therapeutic journal writing

Below are two examples of ways people can sabotage their desire to begin journal writing.

First, the idea that you have to write every day – this isn't the case, but of course the more often you can write the greater the benefit. This is one of the most prevalent myths of journal writing. The journal writing habit has more therapeutic benefit if it is done more often, and if it can be done every day then the benefits increase proportionally. However, not being able to or not choosing to write every day does not invalidate the process, nor undermine the writing that is manageable.

Second, you have to be good at writing and write in 'proper English' – this is also a myth. Spelling, grammar and syntax are all unimportant in journal writing. No one is going to judge you on your writing ability. (It doesn't even have to make sense!)

Key concepts in therapeutic journal writing

This section is important in that it describes the fundamental ideas and approaches that underpin therapeutic journal writing.

Structure, pacing and containment

These concepts are three very important ideas in therapeutic journal writing (Adams 1990).

The practitioner working with other people has a responsibility for the safety of her clients/students/supervisees and for not placing them in situations which could be detrimental to their health and wellbeing.

'What can be dangerous about merely writing?' you might ask. The answer is that writing can take us into deep and dark places and, without structure, pacing and containment, it could become very messy. Use of these concepts will enable you to create a safe and supportive framework in which therapeutic journal writing can take place. When they are in place the writer, whether self (you) or other (your clients, students, supervisees), is given boundaries and a measure of safety which either then allows more profound work to be done or prevents work being done for which they are not ready. In work with other people these boundaries should be established, then built on and reinforced until clients, students and supervisees can provide them for themselves. When working with groups (see Chapter 2, pp.61–5) the establishment of ground rules can be the first step in providing containment; with individuals the contract between practitioner and client does this. Once these ground rules are in place then the choice of journal intervention to match the situation will continue the process.

- **Structure** – The structure of the setting and the relationship is the first external consideration. Groups provide a structured setting and relationships are held within the group. Keeping initial writes short and timed provides an external boundary or structure. But above all structure is provided by the kind of write undertaken. Some interventions are naturally more structured than others (for examples of structured interventions, see Lists, Chapter 4; Captured moments, p.113, Clustering, p.95). Moving from more to less structured exercises in a considered programme of interventions allows people to build up their internal awareness of boundaries and needs, allowing them to develop their own internal structures.

- **Pacing** – Pacing is taking one step at a time towards the destination, making each step manageable, each one leads to the next, strides can be lengthened as muscles strengthen. Rest places can be built in to gather resources before going on – this could mean re-visiting earlier writing or doing more writing of the kind which was found to refresh before. It can also mean building up confidence in writing by starting with simple short exercises before moving on to more extended pieces.

  Choosing the right pace can mean avoiding diving into the deepest, biggest area of experience first but working towards it in stages. Managing levels of fatigue and energy is also an important consideration. Choosing exercises which fit the stage of development and the task which you want to approach is another way of pacing yourself to keep yourself or your clients/students/supervisees safe. For example, beginning with a writing task about the here and now can allow people to enter their own experience in the moment; this can be the first step towards the more difficult or hidden material. Choosing exercises with an emphasis on positive experience can be a way of building up resources to begin work on distressing or painful times.

- **Containment** – Containment is about providing boundaries and limits to contain the experience of self and emotion. This can be provided by the physical material – the book, the pages, and respect for privacy. The book becomes the container to be put away or brought out when required. The edges of the page become containing limits for the writing which would overflow.

Time boundaries become a containing force. In Pennebaker's (1990) writing-about-trauma model participants write for 20 minutes which is felt to be long enough for real disclosure, but not so long that it could be overwhelming. Telling people that they should stop writing after a set time (be that 10, 15 or 20 minutes) gives them permission to stop and is short enough that they can protect themselves from going too far too quickly. On the other hand, a short time can provide a kind of leverage and tension which can make something happen that would otherwise have taken a long time to achieve. This is the same phenomenon as with time-limited therapy which can achieve surprising outcomes because of that very pressure of time. Timed writes within a therapeutic context tend to be shorter than those in creative writing fora.

In groups, containment is provided by the presence of other people and the group cohesiveness which the facilitator has established (Yalom 2005).

Finally, containment is again provided by exercises themselves which can vary from the very containing lists to the least containing act of freewriting.

The feedback loop

This is another integral principle that underpins the practice of therapeutic journal writing. It is one of the things that distinguishes therapeutic journal writing from the purely descriptive.

It involves reading back the material you have written, and then writing a 'feedback statement', providing a reflective response to what you read. In this feedback loop, the self on the page is recognized and the relationship to it is deepened in that moment. Any journal entry can be part of an ongoing reflective process, deepening and developing self-knowledge. The feedback loop also has the benefit of offering a way of structuring every piece of writing.

There are two types of feedback statement:

1. Feedback statements can be about the content of what you've written (or not written):

   • When I read this I am interested that…

   • When I read this I notice…

   • When I read this I remember…

   • When I read this I am surprised to find…

   • When I read this I realize that…

2. Feedback statements can be about feelings evoked as you read your journal entry:

   • When I read this I feel…

   • When I read this I have a sensation of…

   • When I read this I am aware of…

The feelings may be embedded in the written words on the page or they may be registered during the reading.

As mentioned above, to uncover the layers of meaning and insight contained in the journal entry the first stage is to read it. At this point people very often find something that surprises them, and common responses include:

   • 'I didn't know I'd written about that'.

   • 'I didn't know I felt like that'.

   • 'So that's what that's about'.

   • 'Where did *that* come from?'

These illustrate how the individual sees the self on the page in the written words. Sometimes there is something unrecognizable that needs to be re-integrated. The ability to remain open and curious is invaluable in moving things forward and deeper.

These initial reactions are valuable; they can be a source of great insight and personal development. They can also be the first stirrings of recognition and healing and of making connections to the self. Writing both the reactions on reading and further insights gained is enlightening. Feedback statements are a way of capturing this stage, of finding the meaning and making explicit the connections, bringing to consciousness the hidden parts of the self.

Feedback statements are reflections on what has been written and read and can be used after any and every journal entry. They do not have to be done immediately if a period of separation and distance is required. (for an example, see Journal Prompt: The stages of the feedback loop, p.39).

Frances, who attended one of my classes, wrote a description of a memory from childhood of an occasion when she was punished. The writing formed a coherent narrative with period detail, but was somehow devoid of emotion or feeling. As she read it she began to feel a deep sadness welling up from somewhere inside. Her feedback statement was:

> When I read this I am surprised to find that I am getting upset now. I can feel tears welling up and a tightness in my chest; I feel so sorry for the little girl in this piece sent to her room banished from the family – and she didn't even really know what she had done wrong and she was frightened and confused. I want to try and explain things to her – that it wasn't something so terrible.

This began a huge shift in perspective on how she viewed her childhood. As an adult she could recognize that some of the ways her parents had behaved were not entirely healthy. As a child she had only been able to locate the faults in herself.

Another individual with whom I worked, Maya, was receiving counselling and, at the suggestion of her counsellor, wrote an 'unsent letter' which involved writing a letter to her husband after he left her – in doing so, she discovered an empowering anger on the page (for more on Unsent Letters see Chapter 8 p.137). Her feedback statement was:

> When I read this I see how angry I am with you and I can begin to see that this is about you and not about my failure to

be a good wife to you. I am surprised to see the anger on the page – I wonder where it's been until now?

Feedback statements are a way of deepening our relationship with the self, of completing the reflexive loop and beginning the process of re-integration. As part of therapeutic journal practice they increase understanding and learning through further reflection. Feedback statements can be simple and brief, or can lead into more extended journal writing. There are occasions when a feedback statement can lead directly into action. In therapy, the insights from the feedback statements can be the material for therapy rather than the original writing. They bring hidden and crucial issues into conscious awareness.

Catharsis

Catharsis is a particular type of writing without structure; the pace is usually fast and the only 'containment' is the physical page:

> *Cathartic* writing is done under the pressure of intense emotion that calls for immediate expression. It could be as simple a statement as, 'I'm so angry!' or 'I'm crazy about her!' It could be as elaborate as 20 pages of emotional outpouring. (Rainer 1977, p.53)

When people talk about finding their journal writing 'therapeutic' they often actually mean that they find it 'cathartic' – a 'scream on the page' – and many use their journals solely for this purpose – to 'dump'. This type of writing is the venting, ranting and emotional purging which can be useful and necessary at times of great, overwhelming feeling. When engaging in cathartic writing, the journal can become a container for all of those reactions and feelings which threaten to overwhelm and can potentially poison ourselves and our relationships. It is a kind of 'writing in flow' and, by not imposing boundaries, it gives you permission to dump all your feelings on the page. Often, a cathartic rant is the first necessary step in being able to understand and transform those overwhelming states which could prove damaging if allowed to get out into the lived experience and relationships. However, cartharsis alone is not enough; it is only the beginning of a process of understanding and integration.

Cathartic writing followed by the feedback loop can transform journal writing into therapeutic journal writing.

Cathartic writing can be helpful in working with anger management issues – unexpressed anger can build up into a toxic volcano which can erupt with damaging and sometimes irreparable consequences. Exploding on the page is a controlled explosion, and some people destroy their angry rants immediately afterwards. This may be for any number of reasons: because the job is done and the toxin has been removed or defused; because the writer cannot bear to have the reminder of the out of control, or potentially extreme, state; or because destruction of the words on the page is part of the catharsis.

The handwriting in cathartic journal entries can often be identified because it seems to depict some more primitive stream of consciousness – sometimes it gets bigger and bigger during the write; the pen digs tracks in the page, perhaps goes through the paper; lines do not contain or constrain the feelings; all the learned niceties of writing are forgotten and left behind. People often do not recognize their own handwriting in these pieces; it can seem as if it has regressed to an earlier stage of development.

Below is an example of a 'scream on the page'.

> Janet is a single parent who has managed to build up a career, keep the home together and raise two children to university age. She uses her journal as therapy to process her feelings and to contain difficult times. Her son came home for the holidays and after the first couple of days their ability to share a house was compromised by, as she saw it, his messy, slovenly ways. She would come in tired from work to a kitchen full of dirty dishes and hard-to-clean pans. She said, 'I wanted to explode, I was exhausted and my home was no solace comfort.' In her journal she wrote:
>
>> I'm beside myself, incandescent, overwhelmed, I can't bear it. I throw my bag on the floor, and my coat. There's mess everywhere, pans and plates and trails on the table and dirty greasy knives and forks and plates and pans and bowls in the sink on the side.
>>
>> It's not good enough I can't bear it; I want to throw the whole lot out of the door on the floor dirty water mess everywhere I want to throw something and scream and curl up in the corner and disappear and go away. It's so selfish and it's so not fair and I want to scream and SCREAM and SCREAM why should I have this, not fair.

Janet described how cathartic writing would exhaust her rage, get it out of her, return her to a more 'human state'. After a few deep breaths she was able to get up, start cleaning up and talk to her son when he came back later, 'I could talk to him instead of ranting at him which would not have improved the situation. It's just hard when I come home from work, tired and wanting a cup of tea, I know he's not unusual for his age and stage.'

Journal Prompt: The stages of the feedback loop

1. Write your journal entry.
2. Read your journal entry (either silently or aloud).
3. Give yourself some written feedback using one of the sentence stems listed on p.35.

Refer back to pp.34–37 if you want a reminder on how to use the feedback loop.

———•◦•◦•———

CHAPTER 1

Preparing for Therapeutic Journal Writing

In this chapter, I detail the practical considerations that need to be addressed before actually starting a therapeutic journal, including choosing the physical journal itself, finding the right writing tool and thinking about where and when the journal will be written.

The journal

There's a plethora of different blank books for journal writing. For some reason those called journals seem to have ruled pages, whilst the identical books called sketch books have plain pages. There are Fair Trade notebooks with hand-made paper from India, there are business or student diaries and planners, there are leather-bound handsewn volumes from Italy. There are travel journals, reading journals; there are special journals for cooks, gardeners and sporty people. The market for journals is apparently vast.

I prefer notebooks to pre-printed diaries or journals. I choose unlined pages so that my writing can grow or shrink, turn corners or describe spirals or circles or spiders; I can combine writing and drawing at will. However, others prefer lined pages – Rose will not use unlined pages which evoke memories of her school where girls were required to write on plain pages in perfectly straight lines without rulers. For her this is therefore the antithesis of 'freedom to explore'.

Choose the journal which is right for you today

This may be spiral-bound, leather-bound, plain or lined. Choose a book or loose-leaf folder you can use freely and which won't intimidate you or make you feel you can only write 'important things' in it. If you are going to write in confined spaces then a spiral bound book can be useful as it folds neatly back on itself.

Stationery junkies

Many writers of all kinds would confess to this. They have shelves, drawers or cupboards full of beautiful, interesting, inspiring (and mostly empty) notebooks. There is great delight in beginning a new notebook, its fresh clean pages as yet uncontaminated; the unexplored possibilities seem infinite.

Every time individuals or classes discuss the kind of book to use the discussion follows similar lines. It is often agreed that a really nice blank journal is gorgeous, but probably too gorgeous. There are people in every group I've ever facilitated who have a beautiful, probably leather-bound, expensive blank journal waiting for the time when they, their lives and their writing are worthy of such a place.

Some people use ring-binders into which they put every scrap of paper, every written sheet that makes up their journals. They can also include things they have found, cuttings they have read, leaflets and menus, anything of interest; this is a real portmanteau of a journal.

Natalie Goldberg says: 'Choose your tools carefully, but not so carefully that you get uptight or spend more time in the stationery store than at your writing table' (Goldberg 1986, p.7).

Some people keep several journals at the same time and separate out areas of their lives and experiences. They write about different strands in different books and might keep one for dreams, another for work, another for relationships, another for travel. Anna, heroine of Doris Lessing's *The Golden Notebook* (Lessing 2007), kept different aspects of her life in different coloured notebooks – the golden notebook transcended them all and represented her journey towards integration. But as Burghild Nina Holzer says: 'If one separates things out into different notebooks, it is harder to see the larger structure of one's life process, as it slowly evolves over many entries' (Holzer 1994, p.19).

The place

My mother did her accounts at the desk in the drawing room. Apart from this the desk was much polished and dusted, but rarely did anyone sit at it to write. Now I often sit at it to write and rarely dust it. It catches the morning sun in my study as it did in the drawing room of the house where I grew up. I began to write at it after my 'A' levels – when I thought myself grown up enough and important enough.

In my house the sun rises on one side and shines into my study; by the afternoon it has moved round to the kitchen letting the oak kitchen table glow in the light. When there is no one else around I follow the sun; on the rare occasions it's warm enough I'll follow the sun around the outside of the building – or go up the hill and sit on the rocks. Between clients I'll write in my office.

I have spent summers in a house on top of a mountain in Colorado. The sun rises over the plains and sets over the Continental Divide. Sunrise enters the bedroom, ideal for jet-lagged morning pages. During the day there are many writing nooks and perches, inside and out, in sunshine or shade. I like to move around.

I also write my journal in cafes, art galleries or up mountains.

But some people have a special writing place, a place they have carved out of a busy house or a safe space they have created as a sanctuary and that is right for them. Try writing in different places – like different kinds of therapy at different times you never know when a new writing place can be just what you need to open new understanding and make new connections. Writing in different environments can produce different results and help you to access different layers of meaning. It can help you break open your life and break out of routine.

Sometimes writing in public, in a cafe or waiting room, can seem more private than writing at home where the reproaches of the tasks undone can distract from the ability to engage in a relationship with oneself even if there is no one else about. One client, Val, was reluctant to get her journal out when there were other people in the house. She was not just concerned about privacy but found it difficult to focus on herself and her writing in case she was wanted or needed. Being surrounded by strangers who demand nothing of you can paradoxically make you feel alone and not overlooked.

One group member who thought she needed complete solitude to write was surprised to find that writing on a train was extremely productive.

Another client wrote her journal in her car in the few minutes after she'd dropped her children at school and before she returned to housework and studies – this was what she considered to be her time and that she was not stealing it from anyone or anything else which might, as she judged, have a more legitimate call on her. She would then begin to take time to write in her car before and after therapy. Her car became her container and a safe space where she was undisturbed (unless her mobile phone rang – another way in which personal space and privacy can be invaded and few people, it seems, are prepared to turn their phone off in order to write just as clients so often forget to switch them off in a session).

The pen: handwriting or typing?

For some people the fountain pen is the preferred writing instrument. They enjoy the ritual of filling the pen from the ink bottle. Other people might choose coloured pens or different kinds of pen. It is a question of whatever works for you. Some people, of course, like to word process their journals.

Feelings can run high on the subject of whether the 'proper' medium for journal writing is handwriting (with pen or pencil or quill?) or typing.

It can be argued that there is something in the physical process of handwriting which contributes to the therapeutic benefit of journal writing. Writing and the physical movement of the pen over the paper seem to combine to provide a state which is particularly conducive to opening the inner self and allowing emotions to surface.

However, when emotions are very raw, when trauma is still close and thinking about things is close to unbearable then typing can provide an extra layer of safety and defence against the potentially overwhelming nature of the material. For some people, typing is a way of keeping themselves safe when handwriting seems too intimate. Young people, for example, may actually spend very little time writing in consecutive thoughts and for them a keyboard, of one kind or another, is their natural medium.

Some people choose typing over longhand because:

- their writing is illegible even to them

- they type faster than they write and keep up with their thoughts better through typing

- they find that typing allows them to get all their thoughts down without being distracted by the medium

- they believe their journal to be more secure in a password protected cyberspace or hard drive.

Typing allows for invisible editing and correction which creates a different kind of final article – sometimes the Freudian slips lurk in the crossings out or insights can be found in what first was expressed and which remain on the page in a hand-written journal, even if they are heavily overscored. One client of mine called Susan wrote in her journal, 'music from John's room drifts through the sealing.' Surely her unconscious was making some comment about her relationship with her son. Her therapist certainly thought it was worth addressing.

There are many resources and different kinds of software available for electronic journalling and online journal groups have existed for decades. Blogging is an increasingly popular form of recording people's lives and thoughts and interests, but the implications of such unselected sharing have not yet been researched (if reading journals and memoirs can be voyeurism, can blogging be exhibitionism?).

Time

Some people recoil at the idea of writing to time constraints. One of my clients, a therapist called Nick, said he never wrote in timed bursts, he wouldn't like to have imposed time limits, but after writing a five-minute captured moment in the group he reflected and realized that he did in fact set himself limits – he lit an incense stick when he began writing, and stopped writing when it had burned down.

Some people think that creativity and self-expression are antithetical to time boundaries and should never be curtailed or restrained.

However, time limits can make people feel safe, time limits can make journal writing feel manageable. If you know that ten minutes, or even five minutes counts it is very hard to plead time poverty and to make the excuse 'I just don't have time' stick.

> Sometimes one doesn't have time to write. In fact most of the time we don't have time to write. Most of the time we do not have time to be with ourselves. And when that happens, it is time for the five-minute journal entry. (Holzer 1994, p.24)

In groups people are often surprised by how much can be said, or what can be learned in five minutes.

Write every day if you can, don't beat yourself up if you can't

Some people only write in their journals at times of angst or stress. They use their journals as containers for the uncontainable, for ridding themselves of the unbearable or for trying to work through difficult experiences. For them, journals are mainly places of cathartic release and this is their therapeutic function. Such people are often surprised at the idea that journal writing is accessible at other times and that the journal can also be a place of celebration or delight. In this way they learn to look upon their journal as a different kind of therapeutic space.

Some people find that journal writing deserts them at times when they most need it or think that it could be of great therapeutic benefit. After her husband died Annette, a counsellor and regular journal writer, someone with a great appreciation of the therapeutic benefits of journal writing, found she was unable to write about him at all. This felt like a double (but of course not equal) loss. Slowly her ability to write returned; it was mirroring her journey through grief to recovery.

Privacy

One of the most frequently given reasons for not keeping a journal is lack of privacy. Sometimes this stems from earlier experiences of having that privacy violated, but sometimes it is a fear of what might be revealed to the writer. Thoughts happen in the privacy of our own heads, we think them and they vanish; when we write them down they take on a reality which cannot disappear or possibly even be ignored.

Every journal writer is responsible for his/her own privacy and for protecting the privacy and security of the journal. Some people recommend writing on the title page:

> This is the private journal of _____
>
> Please respect my privacy and don't read any further

Annette collected various pieces of writing she'd done about her family and collected them in a folder on which she'd written:

> Read at your peril – you may not like what you find

She said that if they opened the folder after her death then they couldn't say they hadn't been warned.

The Guardian's Saturday supplement, *Weekend*, regularly features a series of one-page articles called 'Experience' in which people are invited to share their experiences. One week it was entitled: 'Experience: I read about my wife's affair in her diary' (*Guardian Weekend* 2009).

The first reaction of the person reading the article might be horror at the violation of privacy perpetrated, and then possibly a thought that he got some kind of just desserts. Eavesdroppers after all never hear any good of themselves and reading someone's journal is a kind of eavesdropping. However, on reading the full article it sounded as though the diary had been left on the (marital) bed: 'This was unusual but, stranger still, it was open.'

The reader's sympathy might begin to shift here – it was as if the husband was being invited to read, provoked to find out the very thing that would hurt him most. His wife used her journal as a weapon.

Sometimes people use this kind of indirect communication to convey difficult things, perhaps even deliberately to cause hurt.

One client, Aruna, was struggling with her housemate's rowdy and untidy behaviour – leaving her journal on the kitchen table may have been her way of trying to tell them that but the effect was not what she wanted. When her housemate Lisa read what Aruna had written her response was not to go and tidy the bathroom but to confront Aruna about her own shortcomings as a housemate. Leaving her journal on the kitchen table meant that of course someone read it and was hurt and angry that she had written these things. In turn Aruna was indignant that the unspoken rule had been broken and they had read her private journal. However, this certainly precipitated some conversations that the housemates had been avoiding.

Louise, a student in a journal group, offered another rationale for not concealing her journal:

> I don't keep my journal out of sight, locked in a drawer or at the back of the books on my shelves, because if I did I would never get it out and write in it. But because I don't conceal it I don't write from my deepest self, because I don't want to confront it, and because, perhaps, I am afraid of someone seeing it. Perhaps that someone is me after all. This is how I sabotage my own intentions.

The responsibility for protecting privacy can extend beyond the grave. Some people leave instructions that their journals should be destroyed or that they should be left to a particular person (often not a family member, but possibly a therapist or close friend).

Another way to protect privacy is not to write anything that would hurt or concern somebody else, but this would contravene the idea that a journal is a private space in which you get to know yourself, warts and all.

My mother kept diaries and after her death I was delighted to inherit them. I wanted to know her better, to understand her more, particularly as we had not always had an easy relationship. However, she did not write them as a therapeutic process. Her early diaries conveyed some of the excitement of a girl at Cambridge and dates and times of her social life, but very little insight into the development of a young and independent woman. Similarly, when she was widowed she began travelling and kept travel journals which are descriptive but entirely external; there is no sense of an inner life or even of significant personal events. She came home from one trip with a proposal of marriage (which she refused, her fidelity to my father's memory was never compromised) but although she mentions having tea with the suitor there is no mention of such a momentous event. It almost seems perverse to use a personal journal in such an impersonal way.

And if my narcissistic hope was to learn more about myself and my place in her life then that was also sorely disappointed. Recently I scanned through some of my old journals and my sense was that they were quite boring and self-indulgent and the recurring themes were stuck in a hopeless loop from which I would never move on. That I think was as much a reflection of the moment of reading as the time of writing – on another occasion I would find much to think about and notice.

Selective sharing

So although the need to protect privacy is very strong there may be times when selective sharing is useful. It is important to consider why sharing seems desirable or useful and what response, if any, is being sought.

You might choose to share part of your journal with your therapist, a family member or the subject of your journal entry. Some forms of journal writing are not intended to be shared – for example, unsent letters, which are explained in more detail in Chapter 8, p.137 are not to be shared with the person to whom they are addressed (although a client who did post a supposedly 'unsent letter' through the letterbox of her ex-husband was threatened with a libel suit).

---•◆•---

CHAPTER 2

Using Therapeutic Journal Writing in Practice Settings

In my workshops on using therapeutic journal writing in practice settings, participants often come with the initial impression that it is simply a process of recording thoughts and feelings. They are then surprised at the breadth of its scope and the range of techniques it encompasses and quickly realize that introducing therapeutic journal writing with clients or students is not an odd or reductive thing to do. Practitioners also often recognize how they themselves can make use of it to support their own personal and professional practice.

Meena, a primary care counsellor, attended one of my training days and said to me afterwards, 'I hadn't realized that what I was doing with some clients has a name, I didn't know it was journalling.'

She had been unknowingly using therapeutic journal writing prompts in her own work, suggesting to some clients that they write unsent letters (Chapter 8, p.137) and to others that they make various kinds of list (Chapter 4, p.89). She also asked others to write down thoughts and feelings but instinctively understood that this was something to be used with care and was not suitable for all her clients at all times. She had intuitively discovered two important things about using journal writing with others:

- It is a useful and effective tool for clients.
- It feels safer when structured.

In my workshops for professionals, participants are asked to complete the following sentence stem:

> When I ask my clients/students/supervisees to write journals they...

The completions below are typical.

- ...sometimes love the idea, sometimes dismiss the idea
- ...often say they are no good at writing or haven't written since school
- ...don't know where to begin
- ...say 'what about?'
- ...worry about details like spelling
- ...would probably be nervous at first
- ...want to know more.

What these seem to suggest is that when introducing journal writing as a new aspect of education or therapy there is a need to understand where the clients/students/supervisees are starting. There is often a level of anxiety which needs to be dispelled. It is therefore important to think about means of providing support, encouragement and understanding or, as previously outlined, structure, pacing and containment (p.32–4).

Practice contexts for therapeutic journal writing

There are three broad categories of context in which practitioners may be working:

- **Educational** – including schools, universities and some adult education settings.
- **Health and social care settings** – including NHS or voluntary sector organizations and private sector work.

- **Creative and cultural industries** – including community groups, social writing groups, libraries and some adult education work.

In each of these, journal writing may be a small part of another curriculum, treatment or programme, or it may exist as itself and occupy its own space. There are expectations and experiences particular to each context.

Therapeutic journal writing in education settings

In educational settings, the work is embedded in an environment where there is already an expectation that work, particularly written work, will be scrutinized, judged and marked.

Therefore it is important when introducing journal work in an educational context to try to ensure that it is not seen in the same way as assignments or projects.

Students, whether on counselling or other courses, often have to keep a learning journal in which to record their experience. For some people this can be a most onerous and uncreative task, even provoking considerable anxiety, but when they realize there are other ways to do it than simply writing analytical, academic prose the task becomes a pleasure rather than a burden.

For example, they can write dialogues with their work, their colleagues, their lecturers, or they can write unsent letters to investigate relationships or clarify misunderstandings (Bolton 2010). They can write songs or poems about their experiences or clusters/spidergrams to plan their work and set their intentions.

Therapeutic journal writing in health and social care

In health and social care settings the introduction of writing may well be met with surprise or resistance, from the organization if not from the client.

Although there is a small but growing body of evidence to demonstrate the efficacy of the practice (e.g. Adams 1999; Morisette 2001; Wright 2009) it is not yet widely known or taken seriously as evidence-based practice in the way that other treatment interventions are. Some professional groups may be sceptical about the therapeutic benefits of journal writing because it has not been subject to much empirical testing or the subject of randomized controlled trials. For these people the results from their own experience of it can surprise them.

Therapeutic journal writing and other forms of expressive writing may well be seen as part of occupational therapy rather than as a separate discipline.

Therapeutic journal writing in creative and cultural settings

In creative and cultural settings there may be expectations of preparing a written product for publication rather than a desire to focus on the process of writing. This expectation can come from both the funders and the students/participants. When I run journal groups in this setting there is almost always one person who comes to the group because 'I want to write my autobiography'. This is of course a valid aim and the group may be of great benefit and help them towards that end; however, the writing, crafting and editing of a publishable work is never the ostensible goal or outcome of the therapeutic journal group. Another group member is the one who comes because he or she wants to write for journals, probably scientific ones; these people often decide they are in the wrong place. Apart from the examples above, people come because they:

- are curious to find out what it is

- don't know what to expect but will give it a try

- know what they want and have a good idea that they'll find it here

- want to deepen their understanding and practice

- keep journals and want to discover new techniques

- want to work on specific aspects of the self.

Introducing therapeutic journal work to others

When beginning to work with journal writing, particularly in clinical settings but also in other places, it is important to remember that many clients are vulnerable people who come to this work at times of stress and difficulty. The work itself can unexpectedly bring up difficult or challenging subjects or aspects of the self, and it can tap into emotional areas that may not have been previously explored. This is true of all writing in all settings – something can be released which can be distressing or moving and everyone who runs writing groups should be aware of this possibility. This can be true for the facilitator as well – your own or other people's process and writing can raise issues for you which you need to think about. These can take you by surprise in the moment and be taken to supervision (see Chapter 12, p.194).

All journal writers, whether clients, students or supervisees, also bring their own personal histories of writing which a facilitator may need to become aware of and to work with – for example, some people may have had negative educational experiences which then have a powerful effect on their subsequent relationship to the written word. It is therefore important to establish with clarity in the journal writer's mind (individually or as a group) that in this work the facilitator is:

- not a teacher

- not the 'expert' on what they or other people around them are writing

and that:

- this is not a lesson

- this is not education (except in the broadest and most personal sense – the experience will, after all, be full of learning)

- there will *not* be a test at the end of it

and most importantly that:

- there is no wrong or right way to do it

- whatever you write is right

- the participant needs to trust the process.

Seamus Heaney once said he trusted that whatever needs to be written will be written, and so can we: trust the process, and the pen.

Facilitators and practitioners need to be clear that in therapeutic journal writing there is no critical judgement on anything which is written. This may be contrary to participants' experience; many people may previously have only written things to be judged, for assessment or scrutiny by teachers, bosses, lecturers or co-workers.

Sometimes it is hard for people to allow themselves to believe that this is 'personal writing' and they themselves may well be the only reader and the only audience these words will ever have (and possibly the harshest critic they could ever have).

It is useful for the facilitator to establish, early on in the process, what someone's previous relationship to and experience of writing has been and to explore their current opinions about writing (one suggestion might be to use the Journal Prompt: My personal history of writing, p.70).

It can be explained at this point that this may be different from their previous experiences with writing and that this writing may not be read to or by anyone else and that it is an entirely personal document. There are many benefits in reading work aloud and having it received by someone else, by other people who are willing to hear and accept your words without judgement (see p.65–69).

Therapeutic journal writing in counselling or psychotherapy

Below is an account of how therapeutic journal writing can be used in the specific practice setting of counselling or psychotherapy. I include this here because there are additional considerations that are useful to bear in mind.

As we have mentioned, some therapeutic modalities do use writing as part of the contract and an activity within therapy. Cognitive behavioural therapy (CBT) regularly uses logs and thought diaries (e.g. Fennell 2001); cognitive analytic therapy (CAT) uses letters between therapist and client (Ryle 2004). Gestalt therapists use the principles of many of the exercises described here but may not go so far as to write them; therapeutic dialogue writing is a version of the empty chair exercise much referenced in Gestalt therapy (Clarkson 2004). Therapeutic journal writing expands the possibilities of writing in therapy and writing as therapy by transcending the therapeutic orientation; it can be usefully introduced as an adjunct to talking therapies whatever the modality (Thompson 2004).

Using therapeutic journal writing in clinical settings can help clients access thoughts, feelings and previously unacknowledged material. This will often be part of the process or even the goal of therapy. It seems that for some people writing something can happen before it can be spoken; it is as if they can write the unspeakable. For example, I have noticed this happening with survivors of child sexual abuse, particularly in cases where there are very high levels of shame and where there have been heavy injunctions of secrecy or 'not telling' in someone's life. Writing things down seems like a private act, a lesser transgression than saying the words out loud to a therapist, almost as if they can still somehow remain silent. Sometimes it is easier to write them than to think them, perhaps because writing is externalizing and not necessarily keeping them. Writing can be a cathartic act (see Cathartic writing, p.37–39). Shame is a powerful silencer; whatever the underlying issue is it can be hard to talk about things which induce feelings of shame. Therapy is often about helping clients face the experiences which they see as shameful and therapeutic journal writing can be a helpful stage in doing so.

Writing in sessions

Writing in therapy sessions can be very helpful for both client and therapist when talking seems difficult – for either physical or psychological reasons. When there really is no voice for physiological reasons (as after voice box surgery, or when a client has a speech impediment) or for psychological reasons (such as when anxiety or trauma result in somatic symptoms), this is when physical symptoms with no apparent physiological cause occur (see Suki, pp.178–9). Therapists need to be aware of whether writing is primarily in the client's interests or whether it is rather for their own ease and comfort.

Table 2.1 Reasons for using journal writing
in a talking therapy session

Physical reasons	Psychological reasons
Somatization resulting in throat/voice conditions	Somatization of psychological material
Permanent physical conditions, e.g. throat cancer	The material is unbearable
Temporary physical conditions, e.g. sore throat, voice strain	The material is unspeakable
Speech impediments, accents, difficulty in communicating through spoken language	The material is beyond the edge of awareness

Introducing therapeutic journal writing in therapy

Practitioners who are new to this work often seem unsure about how to broach it within a counselling context or within psychotherapy which is not explicitly journal therapy.

The introductory question, which may be asked at assessment or at a later point, could be something like: 'I wonder if you've ever thought about keeping a journal?' This tends to open up the discussion more than a question like: 'Have you ever kept a journal?'

The former question will normally elicit people's experience and feelings about journal writing. Many people, more than might be anticipated, respond positively to the idea of journal writing; even those who have had no prior experience or who have never considered it have their curiosity engaged and want to find out more. The number still seems high even when compliance and the desire to please the therapist have been taken into account.

Using the second question may evoke feelings of guilt or discomfort about never having kept a journal (it may be interpreted as implying, 'I should have') or for having given up keeping a diary/journal (implication, 'I shouldn't have stopped, I should have continued, I failed' which is often the curse of the date book again and those reproachful empty pages after the end of January). It may also set up expectations of, 'I should want to and I should understand what is wanted.'

In time-limited therapy I routinely ask the question, 'I wonder if you've ever thought about keeping a journal?' in the assessment session. Developing therapeutic journal writing as a self-sustaining, reflective tool is particularly useful in the context of time-limited work; therapeutic journal writing is the antithesis of time-limited because it is always available, always accessible and ongoing.

Unlike most forms of treatment it is also entirely within the writer's control. Giving someone six sessions of therapy will help them look at a current issue or identify areas for further exploration; this may give them ways of thinking they can apply in the future. Teaching someone to keep a therapeutic journal gives them a tool for life.

Keeping a journal is increasingly something suggested by psychological therapists of many modalities as part of a therapeutic intervention. This could be a structured log, particularly as part of a CBT or solution-focused intervention, often intended to address a particular issue such as eating patterns or occurrence of panic attacks. Sometimes clients will be encouraged to keep a journal to write down all their thoughts and feelings.

This is often where therapists and counsellors begin, that is, by inviting their clients to write in a free-flowing, 'whatever comes into your mind' kind of way. However, this can be too much too soon for some clients, particularly those who are in a borderline state, who might be on the edge of a psychotic episode or who are clinically very depressed. It cannot be stressed too strongly that journal writing must be used with care and that this is extremely powerful work.

Journal therapists or therapists trained in the use of the type of therapeutic journal writing recommended in this book tend to end where many people begin: the freewriting, flow-writing technique is only introduced when we know our clients well and can make a clinical judgement that it will be both safe and beneficial for them. Initially clients are likely to be given more structured tasks; it is important that they are given tasks which match their level of self-awareness and vulnerability. This is again about paying attention and providing appropriate levels of structure, pacing and containment (see pp.32–4).

More structured therapeutic journal writing techniques such as Lists (p.89), Captured moments (p.113) or Steppingstones (p.103) may be more suitable as introductory exercises and for creating manageable exercises than less structured techniques such as Unsent letters (p.137) or

Dialogues (p.127). Some descriptive tasks can be very free-flowing and make good bridges into some of the deeper and unconstrained types of writing.

Setting time boundaries is a way of providing containment and offering people low-risk opportunities to experiment with therapeutic journal writing. Gradually people can move from the more concrete to the more free-flowing exercises and the choice of exercise should keep pace with their development. As you get to know your individual clients or group you will develop a sense of what will be useful and how things will be received.

Using therapeutic journal writing within a session

Whilst writing in counselling and psychotherapy sessions usually occurs between sessions, often as 'homework', there are occasions when it becomes useful to introduce some writing during the session. It is always a question of making a judgement about how the time can be most effectively be used.

Writing within talking therapy sessions would normally only be for short writes, perhaps five minutes, not more than ten. This ensures that there is time for therapist and client to process the activity. Sometimes they will share it and at other times they might simply talk about it. The following are some of the occasions when it can be clinically useful to write in a session; when:

- some insight/realization occurs which it seems important to capture before it evaporates

- it is important to remember something for later

- setting intentions or goals

- 'stuckness' may be preventing the work continuing in the moment

- emotions or feelings are not being acknowledged

- introducing journal writing as a new activity

- formulating journal prompts or topics to write later

- a client has been unable to write between sessions but wants to

- speaking and listening become too hard or exhausting.

Below is an example of how therapeutic journal writing can be used within a session:

Anne:

One day Anne had an 'aha' moment in her counselling session, an important memory surfaced and gave her the sudden realization of her own worth. This came after weeks of wondering why she bothered to exist. She grabbed her pen and journal and immediately wrote the following poem:

> I remember, I remember
> You held me, you comforted me,
> You told me I exist,
>
> I remember now
> The moment when
> Your arms were round me
>
> I was safe
> I was warm
> I was me
>
> Now I know I am
> Because I remember then

Writing in the session enabled her to capture her moment of realization. It also allowed her to create something which she could take away; it provided a written record, the more powerful because it was written in the moment.

The poem contained not only the essence of her self-discovery and the memory she had recovered of being held in her mother's arms as a child, but it also contained the experience of the time and place and the safety of the counselling relationship in which she wrote it. It also allowed her to have her insight witnessed and confirmed by her therapist.

Helpful client factors

Therapeutic journal writing will not be suitable for every client; it is not a universal panacea. In order to identify those clients who are most likely to benefit and who will find it most congenial there are certain characteristics we can identify (Adams 1999).

When any of the following are present the evidence suggests that a positive outcome in the use of journal writing in therapy is more likely so that it becomes therapeutic journal writing:

- *Prior experience of keeping journals/diaries*: if people are already familiar with the concept and experience of keeping a diary or journal, particularly if it was a useful or positive experience, then they will take more easily to the idea of using journal writing for therapeutic purposes.

- *Motivation*: clients who are motivated to change are likely to be more open to trying new and different ideas. They are willing to try something to see if it works.

- *Commitment*: a commitment to themselves and to the process of therapy will help clients begin to commit to the ongoing process of keeping a therapeutic journal.

- *Positive relationship with writing*: people who have had a positive relationship with writing, often from their early educational settings, or from their professional lives, will be pre-disposed to undertake therapeutic tasks which involve writing.

- *Strong relationship with the facilitator*: a strong relationship with their facilitator will pre-dispose clients to look favourably on their suggestions. Research has shown that the relationship is the key factor in therapeutic change.

Caveat

Freewriting, flow-writing can be a dangerous tool with vulnerable people. The instruction or suggestion: 'Write down your thoughts and feelings, whatever comes into your head,' should be uttered with the utmost caution.

Structure, pacing and containment are even more important with vulnerable populations. Freewriting should only be suggested to clients/patients when it seems clinically safe, usually after a structured programme of other journal writing exercises.

Contraindications

It can be inadvisable to use writing:

- where clients are in danger of becoming psychotic

- where people's grasp of reality is challenged

- where there is poor impulse control

- when someone is so depressed that the effort to write is more than they can bear – and becomes yet another failure.

However, when you can trust clients to manage their boundaries and keep themselves safe, and they can trust the process and allow what needs to be written to be written, then you have the basis for a relationship with therapeutic journal writing.

Working with groups

Group facilitation is primarily about providing safety (Field 2006). If you are facilitating a group of individuals who are engaging in therapeutic journal writing, there are various questions for you to consider before the first meeting.

Ground rules

At the first meeting, all groups should cover and negotiate the basic ground rules for the group which might include:

- Confidentiality – what is revealed in the room should stay in the room.

- Communication should always be respectful which means things like not interrupting or speaking over each other.

- Group members should not be critical, judgemental or offensive about each other or about each other's writing.

- There is never any requirement to read what you have written.

- Participants are responsible for managing their own level of disclosure. Whilst the facilitator is responsible for safety in the group, participants are responsible for what they choose to write about and to share. It may be appropriate for the facilitator, perhaps in the early stages of a group coming together, to say: 'This can be a powerful exercise, you may not wish to write about the most important or the most emotionally loaded subject this time.'

Facilitators may also want to discuss communication between sessions:

- Between group members – the group can make an agreement that if this happens it will be disclosed and brought back to the group. This can avoid later misunderstandings: for example if a sub-group meets to write together or strong friendships develop which can have implications for confidentiality or group dynamics.

- Between facilitator and group members – there are boundary issues which need to be considered. Some facilitators are happy to be contacted between sessions but put a limit on what can be expected in return – an e-mail from a participant may be acknowledged but not responded to, phone calls regarding practical issues such as attendance may be welcomed but not on other topics. Sometimes participants may ask the facilitator to look at other pieces of writing they have done; this is usually beyond the remit of the relationship within the group, but could be negotiated as a separate activity or suggestions made about where else the writing could be taken.

The role of the facilitator – to write or not to write?

This is an important question for every facilitator to think about: 'shall I join in the experience of writing in a group?' This can seem so tempting, particularly if the exercise appeals to where you are in your own process at the time and if you are struggling in the midst of a busy life to find time to do your own journal writing (it may be useful to refer to Journal Prompt: If I so want to write... p.70).

For some facilitators it can seem like a way of being a more egalitarian facilitator and of 'sharing' in the group experience. Every facilitator must decide this for him or herself, of course, according to the kind of group and the dynamics within it. A peer group is one group in which all members will probably write, even if one of them is holding time-keeping responsibilities, or the responsibility for other boundaries.

Writer and creative writing facilitator Jane, said she initially wanted to do the writes with the group but came to realize that she needed the time to stay with the group process and be clear about her own role. Rob, a psychiatric nurse, wanted to use therapeutic journal writing with his patients; he ensured he'd spent some time trying the prompts before the session.

Groucho Marx is alleged to have said, 'I refuse to join any group that would have me as a member.' Perhaps the similar sentiment applies here: 'I wouldn't facilitate a group that I'd prefer to be a participant in.' Facilitation requires a different kind of attention from being a participant.

The facilitator holds the responsibility for the group. Whilst the group is writing the facilitator needs to have enough attention available to be aware of what is happening in the room, including the dynamics and activity of the group and individuals. This includes noticing things like:

- Whether people are writing or not. Often there is someone who finishes every write earlier than the rest of the group, is it a pattern? Is there someone who never wants to stop? What kind of resistance is being demonstrated? Which exercises engage which group members?

- If there's someone who is struggling or becoming outwardly emotional or upset: do they need permission to take time out? What do they want to bring to the group? What can the group do to support them?

Time while the group is writing allows the facilitator:

- to observe the level of intensity or engagement in the group

- to know them better and to take care of them – this may not necessitate action but will be information which can help the facilitator contain the group process

- to think about how things should proceed in the rest of the session

- to make notes about the group

- to complete necessary administration or record-keeping.

So on the whole as a facilitator I would choose not to write with the group – though of course there may be exceptions with particular groups and on particular occasions. When a group member had to leave because of serious illness the others carried out a series of exercises to help them process the transition and their grief. These resulted in written testimonials to their erstwhile colleague, celebrating her participation. This was one occasion when the facilitator found it beneficial to share in the writing process. The group sent a collaborative piece of writing to her family.

Facilitators will often have experienced the exercises they are facilitating, perhaps many times.

These techniques may be a regular part of your own journal practice, perhaps you learned them in a group or session you attended as a participant or perhaps it was part of your preparation for the current group to do them. It is always useful to have tried out the exercises before you introduce them to others; they can be powerful and you are less likely to be taken by surprise by reactions in the group if you have a sense of where they might lead. In addition, they offer the opportunity for your own personal growth and self-knowledge, sometimes unexpectedly. Experimenting before the session can alert you to where surprises might occur for other people and how particular exercises might unexpectedly get to the heart of the matter.

Some facilitators use the time to write individual prompts for participants based on what they have noticed individuals are working with or not attending to at the moment. These prompts can be done either in the session or at home.

The facilitator may choose to write and speak – to write about what she is observing and to use the opportunity to reflect on her own process and on the group.

During one group exercise I wrote:

And so they write – pens now flying over the paper after a brief hiatus at the beginning. Did I go into it too quickly? Did they need a bit more guidance? But they are certainly writing now.

K looks really angry, face screwed up – I know now that it is her look of concentration, she doesn't really hate me or the world or even what she's writing.

C still struggles hard to find the words; he's writing jerkily.

M writes fast, I can see her going deeper, tears moisten her eyes, she'll be the last to stop.

J is the first to stop – always. I wonder how I can help her get more in touch with this work? She looks covertly around the group and I see her vulnerability – more esteem-building prompts needed.

This is intense – the atmosphere deepens as the group writes and seems to bring them together, you can almost feel the resistance evaporating. They are united in activity.

The facilitator may say things while the group writes. This might include offering a further prompt which will help participants to go deeper, to allow them to access the next layer in their emotions or experience. For example: In a Dialogue (p.127) the facilitator might say: 'Before you bring this to a close, just check whether there is anything else that needs to be said.' or 'Ask your dialogue partner: What do you want from me?' In a Captured moment (p.113), 'What is the feeling tone in the memory you are describing?' In an Unsent letter (p.137), 'Is there anything else at all which you want to have said to this person which you haven't yet said?'

Reading aloud

Although therapeutic journal writing produces an intensely private document and process, selective reading is a significant act which can contribute greatly to the therapeutic process and to the understanding of self and others, and can be used in one-to-one or group settings.

There is something immensely powerful and affirming about reading your journal entries aloud; to hear your words spoken, for them to be sent out into the world somehow makes them exist in a different way. Even reading your journal entries aloud to yourself in solitude allows you to hear what you've written in an entirely new way and to take your words back into yourself and possess them and all their meanings again. This can be the beginning of the process of integration and acceptance.

Progoff encourages reading aloud in groups but reminds us to:

> Bear in mind that the reason for reading...in the group is not at all so that you can tell your life story to the other participants. Your purpose is not to communicate with the others, but to feed back into yourself the experiences of your own existence. (Progoff 1975, p.110)

Initially people may be reluctant to read their words aloud in a group. The first person to do so in any group is owed a debt of thanks by the facilitator and the rest of the group; it can feel very exposing to be the first. At the beginning of the group the facilitator can say that there will be times when participants will be offered the opportunity to read and that this is an invitation not a requirement. The message that 'sharing is optional' should be clearly and regularly iterated. Nobody should ever feel obliged to read; they should understand that 'It's OK to pass'.

There may be times when something is so new or so surprising or painful that the writer needs time to synthesize it or get used to it. My experience is that in an ongoing group, most of the time, everybody in the group will probably have accepted the opportunity to read something, however short, by about the third week. Sometimes people would rather talk about what they have written rather than read it and the facilitator may encourage them simply to read without interpretation, explanation or apology. The prophylactic, 'It's not very good but I'll read it anyway,' comes easily to many people and is probably indicative of either their educational experience or other self-esteem issues. I know it's how I feel when I'm surrounded by poets.

Before the group begins to write, on each occasion the participants should know whether or not there will be an opportunity for them to read what they have written, and also whether or not the piece of writing will be shared.

After a group has spent time writing, the facilitator should be clear about whether everyone will have the opportunity to share their writing or whether there is only time for one or two people to read on this occasion. People take different lengths of time to be ready to say 'I'll read'; if they are waiting to be number four or five and opportunities to read stop after one or two, people can be left feeling somewhat let down, or even rejected and ignored.

There should also be time for adequate response after someone has read. When personal and perhaps difficult or uncomfortable material has been accessed and shared the writer needs to be contained by the group and not left with an overspill of feelings needing to be processed.

Reading aloud can allow emotions to be recognized in a new way and can help someone to know what they are experiencing. Drawing again on the example mentioned on pp.36–7 of Maya, who wrote an unsent letter to her husband after she discovered he was having an affair, she read it out to the group and as she read her voice became angry, she spoke more quickly and more strongly. This marked a real transformation from the hurt and bewildered woman who had previously spoken. Somehow she had written her own script in the letter and was then putting the authentic feeling into the reading.

When talking about it earlier in her counselling session she was still censoring her feelings and almost adopting a different role, a socially acceptable role, the role women like her were 'supposed to play'. Reading aloud gave her access to those underlying angry feelings; writing alone had not allowed her to express or process them. The group was able to hear her read and witness her anger. They did not have to say much in response but she felt fully heard and supported by them.

To have your words received by an other or others is to feel yourself being received and heard in a different way. In therapeutic journal groups or in one-to-one therapy this is an important and dynamic part of the process. Writing and reading in a community, in a supportive environment, is a powerful therapeutic experience. When your words are received by an accepting and non-judgemental audience, it is a most affirming experience. This kind of witnessing is almost a way of confirming existence.

Responding

Responding as a therapeutic journal writing facilitator

As a therapist or facilitator in a one-to-one or group situation it is important to think about the different ways of responding when someone reads from their personal journal. Here are some recommendations:

- Try to be sensitive to the feeling in the room.
- Try to listen contemplatively and attentively.
- Notice your own internal responses.
- Don't respond too quickly (allow the words to settle in reader and listener).
- Respond without judgement.
- Be attuned to the feeling level.
- Reflect the feeling in the words and the voice (notice disparity between the two).
- Ask for clarification of your own impressions.
- Ask gently.
- Try to gauge what the reader wants from you and the group. (You can ask this either before or after someone reads.)

And a couple of caveats:

- Never comment in a 'lit. crit.' way, that is, commenting on style, structure or form of a piece (that is not the task of a group where the focus is on process rather than product writing).
- Never be 'the expert' on someone else's journal writing.

Group responses

How the group responds when individuals choose to share their writing should be discussed and negotiated. Points for the group to consider include:

- What kind of response do you think is appropriate and desirable? What kind of response is invited?
- Before the reader begins ask yourself, 'What do you want from the group?' or, 'What would you like the group to do?'
- Is it right to comment on style or level of writing?
- Is it right to comment on content?

Each group and facilitator will find their own ways of managing these issues. Whether journal writing is being introduced as part of some other activity, whether you are the facilitator or the student, client or group member, it is a joint endeavour in which people are finding a voice.

Ensure that the group understands that a therapeutic journal writing group is a personal and expressive writing group not a creative writing workshop. A therapeutic journal group is not a therapy group, even though it will have therapeutic outcomes, and participants who may require therapy should be referred as appropriate. If a group participant is in therapy it is recommended that they tell their therapist about the group; things may emerge in the group that need to be taken back to therapy. A group of this kind sits on the continuum of creative writing and writing therapy, holding a space between creative writing and writing therapy.

If our premise remains that writing is both a therapeutic act and a creative act, in a therapeutic journal group both aspects come to the fore as people open up to their own and other people's experiences and emotional presence. This is not to say that these issues will be absent from creative writing groups.

Where a creative writing facilitator understands how to work with a group, the outcomes can be decidedly therapeutic.

Facilitators of creative writing groups can be surprised by what is uncovered or unleashed in such an apparently benign setting. In all situations in which creative writing is being produced it is desirable, if not essential, that the facilitator has access to supervision – your own journal can provide you with a measure of self-supervision (see Chapter 12) but cannot completely provide you with the kind of container you may need.

Counsellors and psychotherapists will of course already have their own supervisors who may be able to supervise this kind of work as well as their regular therapeutic practice. If this is not the case it will be important to seek out someone who can provide the necessary level of support and enquiry within the context of an ongoing relationship.

Journal Prompt: If I so want to write...

If I so want to write in the group I facilitate, what is it that needs to happen in my life to allow me the space for this kind of writing? Where can I best do my own writing?

Journal Prompt: My personal history of writing

The first thing I can remember writing is...

My early experiences of writing were...

When I was at school I wrote...

The thing I most enjoyed writing...

A list of the things I have written in the last week:

PART TWO

Structured Techniques

CHAPTER 3

Beginnings and Endings

You've got the book, you've got the pen, you've got/made/found the time, you sit down and... The first blank page imperturbably looks back. The question that comes to mind is: 'Right, so what do I write? How exactly do I begin?'

For novices, the idea of starting to journal, of becoming someone who journals, can be daunting because it represents a step into a new and unknown future self. Even more experienced diarists or journal-keepers can find starting a new journal, a new volume or a new technique daunting. At times even starting a new journal entry can be daunting. Emotions may already be stirring and it is worth paying them some attention (for more on this, try Journal Prompt: Beginning, p.87).

Beginning therapeutic journal activity

I often introduce the ideas by saying:

> Your journal is an extension of yourself; it is a container for all your thoughts, feelings and experiences. This makes it a space for you to enter and fill with whatever is important to you; use it to explore your deepest thoughts and feelings or to process particular aspects of your experience.

Making a conscious transition into the writing place can be helpful, just as a counselling session is different from a spontaneous conversation because it has boundaries of time and place, writing a therapeutic journal entry can be separated from other activities.

This also allows for a demonstration of self-respect. There are times when it seems difficult to step away from the demands of other people, activity or duty. One client, Val, who is the mother of two small children, said it was only when she locked herself in the bathroom that she could find space for herself. For a while her journal lived in the airing cupboard, layered in with the towels.

Sometimes a physical ritual is helpful, such as:

- clearing a space on the desk or table

- doing a few exercises

- making sure the door is closed

- lighting a candle or incense stick

- making a cup of tea.

At other times a more mental calming is helpful, such as:

- a meditation

- a few deep breaths or stretches

- saying a prayer, poem or mantra.

Guided visualizations make good transitional processes. These are stories which use imagery and metaphor to lead people into their inner worlds. An external facilitator can use them with individuals or groups, but they can also be used as self-directed exercises, either by listening to a recording or reading them aloud.

A storytelling workshop I attended began with a guided visualization of going through a door. The facilitator bade us close our eyes and imagine a door, which she then led us through. At the end of the workshop we closed our eyes and the facilitator guided us back through the door, we closed it behind us and were ready to re-enter the outside world and our other lives, crossing a metaphorical liminal space (see Journal Prompt: The door, p.87). Some people negotiate with family or housemates to have protected time for writing during which they are not to be disturbed.

Whilst preparation is important and helpful when conditions allow, there are other times when the only way to enter the journal is to seize pen and paper and start writing wherever you are – on the bus, in the waiting room, on top of a mountain. At these times whatever you write on (bus ticket, menu, napkin, envelope) or with (pen, pencil, lipstick, chalk) is your journal of the moment and the place to capture insights, thoughts and moments which can be developed and processed later. Not writing because you don't have the right pen, book or place is a familiar method of self-sabotage.

Techniques for overcoming the first blank page

Some people like to introduce themselves to their journal. This seems particularly true of adolescent girls and represents part of their search to discover who they are.

Adolescence is a time when the individual identity is still somewhat fluid and even elusive. Keeping a journal can be a valuable part of the search for identity and discovery of the self; it is therapeutic to explore and try on different ideas, selves and identities in the safety and privacy of the journal. Adolescent journals are not simply hysterical outpourings about love objects and self-loathing.

Learning journals introduced at school or college may be the first time that people are asked to keep a journal; the experience can be made less threatening and overtly 'educational' (with all that that may connote) by beginning with something very personal rather than launching straight into the learning experience.

One client, Gwen, wrote:

January 1st 1995

Well, here I am. I'm Gwen, I'm 15 and I'm a schoolgirl. I live here with my younger brother, Charles. He's a pain and I must make sure he NEVER EVER sees this diary. I live with my parents and they would never look at my diary. I'm going to try and write every day so that I don't lose anything. I want to experience fully everything that happens to me. This diary will be my constant confidante as I go through this year.

Naming the self on the page confers identity; becoming the first-person narrator of our own stories begins to establish the continuity of the self and the construction of the individual narrative within a context of time and social networks. Such an 'ordinary' activity in the context of a therapeutic journal may indicate the beginning of self-actualization or emergence of the self.

Dear Diary…

Some people like to personify their journals, to create a named recipient for their words. The 16-year-old Anne Frank (Frank 2009) named her diary Kitty and made her a confidante whose opinion she valued. Some people simply write their journal entries to, 'Dear Diary…'

There are of course times when an omniscient narrator, a third-person observer, can be brought into the journal to provide reflection and perspective; the diary itself can speak, but at the beginning we can step straight onto the pages of our own life.

Dialogue with a new book

One client who was a long-time journal-keeper, Simone, wrote a dialogue (see p.127) every time she started a new volume. She said this grounded her in her life and in her journal and prepared hers for the next phase, whatever it is. This is another kind of transition.

Simone: Hello New Journal.

Journal: Hello Simone, welcome to my pages.

S: Thank you. You are so beautiful and so smooth and I love your creamy blankness. I see you as waiting for me and being open to me but I'm also a bit scared.

J: What are you scared of?

S: I'm scared of spoiling you, of not being able to do you justice.

J: Oh, Simone, whatever you give me and put on my pages will be a privilege to me. I want to receive whatever you want to give me.

S: Thank you, I'll try.

J: What do you want from me?

S: I think I just want that — for you to be there and to hold me and to allow me to write whatever I need.

J: That's what I'm here for. I'm looking forward to getting to know you.

Simone explained that: 'Every journal is different and each one has its own character. I always feel humble and excited when I start a new book — I'm a bit of a stationery junkie at heart and every book that I acquire has called to me.'

Focused journals

Some people journal with a particular and explicit aim in mind. For example, 'I want to write a journal in order to...

- ...get to know myself better'
- ...create a record/legacy/memoir for my children/grandchildren'
- ...reflect on things that happen in my life'
- ...work on a particular issue'
- ...resolve a specific matter'
- ...understand my family/myself/my relationships better.'

With such a focused approach, the way to begin may appear obvious. If journal writing is part of a therapeutic intervention where there are identified therapeutic goals then the starting point is often clear. It may be negotiated with or suggested by a therapist as in the following examples, all of which describe clients who were seen for counselling in a primary care setting.

> Alan, a 25-year-old man, was referred for counselling because he was becoming very socially isolated. He was unable to make contact with people and afraid to go out in case he was mugged. At work he moved to the night shift in the call centre where he worked to minimize his contact with others. In his initial assessment it appeared that his

behaviour started to change after the death of his father four years previously (this event had not been mentioned by the GP in the referral letter). His therapist thought that unresolved grief issues were a real possibility.

His suggested task was to write an unsent letter (p. 137) to his father.

Goal: to begin to grieve for his father, to mourn in a conscious way, to think about his father and recover memories from before the time when his father became ill.

Susan was very depressed. Her life had shrunk to a grey haze and her lethargy, apathy and anhedonia made it difficult for her to do anything or even to see the point of anything. She did manage to attend her counselling appointments most weeks – but there was nothing to sustain her in between.

Her suggested task was to begin a gratitude journal (p. 183) and record two gratitudes each day. Because everything seemed so difficult, the negotiated task needed to be structured and contained enough to be manageable even on her worst days.

Goal: to begin to see something each day which was not annihilated by the pall of depression and to connect one day to another, to begin to construct an ongoing thread of narrative in her experience.

Brenda had battled with her weight throughout her adult life. Now she really wanted to lose weight and to feel healthier but she didn't know why it always seemed such a struggle. She wasn't even sure why she ate so much and so many of the kind of things which sabotaged her desire and ability to lose weight.

Her suggested task was to keep a food journal. In this she recorded not just what and when she ate and but also data about who was there, what was happening before she ate, what she felt before and after eating. She also thought about whether she was ever aware of feeling hungry. In fact she was to record anything which was on the periphery of her eating which could place it in a wider context.

Goal: to understand her patterns of eating and to identify possible triggers which propelled her to eat at particular times, as a result of specific situations, conversations or behaviour.

For some people, perhaps those in the examples above, the process of therapeutic journal writing could be very short-lived and time-limited, but the product can be life-changing.

If it is linked to another kind of intervention, they may both end at the same time. People may feel that the process is completed when the initial goal has been reached and therefore the task has been accomplished. At this point they may decide that they have no further use for their journals. Most people, however, will find that journalling is an open-ended process. Alan used his journal to develop his creativity and began to make significant changes in the direction of his life. He went from working in the call centre to photography and registered for a university course.

People may dip in and out of it but they know that, henceforth, therapeutic journal writing is always available to them. It can be part of their healing and growth whenever they need it.

Once Brenda realized the efficacy of the method, she knew that it was something she could use again if the old patterns in relation to eating and her weight re-asserted themselves. A positive experience of the therapeutic potential of journal writing in therapy or as a self-guided process at a particular time of life will allow people to understand its benefits and how to use it in the future. Many people become converts and integrate journal writing into their lives, adopting it as an ongoing, fluid process, a reflective practice and an important part of their experience.

There may be times when the ability to journal and write desert a client (as in Annette's case, mentioned earlier on p.45). This may be after a trauma, a deep loss or bereavement; a rupture in their narrative. They may suddenly find that, just when they most have need of these tools, they are no longer available to them. There may also be times when resistance to writing about a particular issue or in a particular form is so strong that all writing becomes impossible. At such times, patience can help it to return.

One former client called Mo came week after week to his therapy sessions saying: 'I still haven't written that unsent letter to my mum – I know I need to, I just can't seem to do it.' Although we talked about why it seemed so difficult and why he felt it was so important to do it, nothing seemed to shift anything for him or allow him to take the action he believed would help. Then one week he came in with the letter written; he smiled as if a weight had been lifted, proud of his achievement he presented it to me. I asked him to read it to me. That was the week he ended therapy.

In this case it seems as if Mo's resistance to writing the letter was connected with his unconscious need for therapy and he was reluctant to do anything that might bring his sessions to an end. He feared that if he wrote the letter I would consider the case closed. When he was ready to end therapy he was able to write the letter – the literal task of writing the letter was also a symbolic act and statement of independence.

Themed journals such as eating journals or gratitude journals or other single topic or task-orientated journal activity provide the structure, pacing and containment to encourage someone to begin therapeutic journal writing in a safe and manageable way.

As confidence in the process and in your ability to carry it out increase you may feel empowered to experiment and to step out into other areas of journal writing and thus into the exploration of other areas of the self. Moving from a more structured activity to a more fluid one can be a parallel process with the development of the self.

More prompts for getting started

The first journal workshop I ever attended with Kathleen Adams at The Center for Journal Therapy was a one-day course called 'Journals Quick and Easy'. The day began with a short write for which the prompt was:

Who am I?

Why am I here?

What do I want?

The group responded in as many different ways as there were members.

Since that day, I have used this exercise to open talks, seminars and workshops. It is a useful way of allowing a group to begin by writing, to feel the voice on the page before hearing their voices in the room, beginning a dialogue with the self before beginning a dialogue with others. I have also addressed it countless times in my own journal practice. A former student of mine says she still uses this prompt whenever she starts a new book.

The beauty of these three deceptively simple, or highly complex, questions is that they can be responded to in many ways and on many levels (from the literal, concrete and present to the existential, abstract, timeless and universal). People can connect to them in whatever way feels appropriate at the time, from wherever they are in their experience. Sometimes one of the three will take the writer's attention more than the others. In groups a typical reflection on this might be:

I only got as far as the first one...

or

I didn't think I'd write much but then I ran out of time and there's so much more I want to say.

The answers will be different each time these questions are addressed.

Collecting opening prompts

Amassing a collection of journal prompts is another way to ensure that there is always some way to begin.

Because there is not always time to reflect or write when ideas arise or, when there is time, the subject can prove elusive, having a list of prompts or 'springboards' (Adams 1990) is useful. In addition to your own list, Natalie Goldberg's exercise 'Writing off the page' (Goldberg 1986) involves opening at random any book on your bookshelves and using what you find there as a starting point.

Keep a page (or pages) in your journal to list your starting points. The list can include:

- Quotations – whatever you read, hear or remember.

- Issues in your own life that you feel may warrant further attention.

- Relationships and people.

- Memories or thoughts which suddenly arise when you are thinking about something else but which you know you'd like to return to.

- Themes – the recurring threads in your life.

- Questions which intrigue you.

- Things overheard or observed.

- Things you are told.

Put anything on this list which catches your interest and which may offer you further opportunity for reflection and exploration. If you are working with other people, encourage your students/clients to note things. When you need something to begin a journal entry, look at your lists and pick an item (either at random or one which seems to speak to you at that moment). Begin by committing to it for five minutes (doing so provides a form of containment) – if you want to go further carry on, if not choose another item from the list.

Everyone has things they prefer not to write about and the therapeutic benefit of writing about them may have to wait; just as in talking therapy it can take a long time to get to the deeper issues, even when we know what they are. If the difficult issues can be acknowledged and named, they can be addressed at a future date.

Keep a list of things you won't write about, things that may seem too big, too personal, too painful or boring or dangerous. You never know when a shift will occur which means you can explore them – if they are on this list they are almost certainly worth your time at some point; it may be that you are just not ready to address them. Review this list periodically (either alone or with your therapist if you have one) to measure the extent of your current resistance and note any shifts or changes.

Some people choose to use the back pages of their current journal for this collection of prompts – sometimes they transfer the list from one volume to the next, while other people prefer to start a new list each time. Some people choose to keep them in a separate file on the computer or on looseleaf pages. One client, Dana, always kept hers on her Blackberry so she always had them to hand. Tell your clients: 'This is your stash – bury it where you can find it when you need it.'

Clearing a space

Start where you are, by clearing a space so you can see where you are. This might mean literally and physically clearing a space to write, on your desk, on your kitchen table, or it might mean clearing a space in your mind to begin to write. Listing is one of the journal writer's forms of de-cluttering.

Write a list of all the preoccupations at the forefront of your mind, all the 'to do' lists, the decisions to make, the actions to take, the things to think about (see Journal Prompt: What's really going on… p.87 for more on this). Put down on paper everything preventing you from getting to the things you want to write about. Once these are on the page the items on this list can be re-considered. Do they have any merit as immediate journal material? If not they can be parked on the page to be dealt with later. When the space has been cleared it is possible to notice what is really going on and this can be the place to begin.

Start where you are

Talk about the weather. When I do telephone consultations with someone in another place we always start by comparing notes on the weather outside our respective windows.

It's a grounding conversation which brings us into contact with each other's reality but also acknowledges difference in context. In your journal the weather is another way of connecting to where you are. It can also be a way of identifying patterns and trends in the past. One former client, Robert, kept a summer holiday journal every year from the age of 12. He went to the same place for more than 20 years. The weather in his diary provided a kind of continuity for him and his family to look back on with great interest. Childhood summers are not always the halcyon days of eternal sunshine that perfidious memory would have us believe, but neither were rainy days always disappointments. Robert's diaries became the repository for the family history, a kind of collective memory and Robert became the family archivist to whom others could refer – 'Robert, when was it we…?'

Describe what you can see, hear, smell, feel; as with writing about dreams, writing about the sensory details can increase recall and sharpen experience. Go on to think about movement, temperature and texture as well. (For more, see Journal Prompt: What do you feel now? p.88.)

Use pictures and photographs

Pictures and photographs offer another way into experience and the self. Personal photographs from your own life or the family archive can connect you to other people again or be the source of further work (see section on Working with photographs, pp.116–20).

Photographs or pictures from art can act as springboards in the same way as quotations (see Journal Prompt: Looking at a picture, p.88).

Start with stuckness

Write about what it's like to be stuck, what it's like to have writer's block.

Referring to ideas in Julia Cameron's *The Artist's Way Morning Pages Journal* is a great way to overcome stuckness (Cameron 1997). She advises people to fill three journal pages with whatever comes to mind (containment is provided by the page limit). If you get stuck, just repeat what you last wrote until something else occurs to you and you are ready to move on. This may result in three pages of 'I can't do this, nothing to say.' That may be what you need to do and may reflect where you are – don't be put off by that or by the thought 'it's boring' – just write it down.

The last sentence of the previous journal entry can become the first sentence of the next write which offers continuity into the present. Summarizing what you notice when you read the previous entry has a similar effect.

Ending a journal

What is there to do at the end of a journal? It is not obligatory to write on the final pages. There is no rule which says, 'I must fill this book before I go to the next' (whatever the puritan 'waste not want not' maxim declares). It can be therapeutic and empowering to make the choice to move on. You can leave a journal because your work is done, because you no longer wish to keep it or because you want to start another. There are many good excuses and reasons for starting a desirably new journal – these may include departures from the diurnal round or changes of direction such as:

- going on a trip or moving house
- life transition stages including:
  - having children

- children leaving home

- new relationships

- endings or losses

- personal or professional changes

- beginning a new year/decade/millennium.

Another excellent reason for starting a new journal is simply finding the perfect next journal book and being impatient to set pen to its beautiful pages, wanting to let it contain the next stage of your life.

There can be advantages and opportunities for reflection and learning in declaring a journal finished before the last few pages are filled. The final blank pages can be used in a variety of ways. Just as the feedback loop can be used for a single entry, the technique can be applied to a whole volume or journal period. Before embarking on the feedback loop for a notebook, it is a good idea to number the pages for ease of reference and identifying particular points.

Using the feedback loop for a whole journal

Find a suitable time, long enough for you to read the whole notebook in one sitting so that your feedback is global, covering all the contents. Feedback statements at this time may include:

- a list of recurring themes

- the cast of people (living or dead) who figure in the pages and your reflections on your relationships with them

- the emotional journey you read in the journal

- transition points or shifts

- patterns of thought or behaviour

- unfinished business

- dream material.

Some people choose to write only on either the right- or the left-hand pages throughout and then use the blank pages to comment on what they've written and highlight themes or points. Others leave the last few pages of each journal for a review of the contents – indexing themes, summarizing shifts or stuckness. This is a useful way of recognizing the patterns of the recent past and when done over time can help to track the cycles, trends and blocks in our experience. In times of healing and recovery re-reading old journals can help us to mark the distance travelled and be aware of shifts that have occurred.

Uses for the last blank pages include:

- **Indexing:** develop your own taxonomy in whatever way seems helpful. This could include:

  - themes

  - people

  - moments of change

  - places you've written or written about.

- **Sketching:** draw an image or picture to sum up the journal.

- **The feedback loop:** your reflections on what you find in the journal and where you are.

Below are some journal entry extracts written by former clients which show different useful ways to think about ending a journal.

Saying farewell to the journal: Simone

> It's time to say goodbye, journal, thank you for being open to all the words I've poured into you over the last four and a half months. You kept your word to me and I gave you my words. I shall look back on this time and remember writing in the Purple Onion, writing in Whitby and most of all writing here at my desk. Thank you.

Looking backward, looking forward, writing about where you are: Jenny

> A beastly foot stamping way of ending really. I'm cross and then some – cross that this book is ending now just when I need it. But seeing emptiness in front. Also cross that I am taking my crossness into the new book which will begin contaminated. I'm cross that I'm cross.

> Perhaps I don't have to be – perhaps the emptiness of the new book is potential space for something new. I don't want to end this book

on this sour note – it's not all like that really – I'm cross now but it will pass – it always does – I can smell the honeysuckle. Goodnight.

Re-reading old journals

Re-reading old journals, diaries or letters (a consequence of growing older is that sometimes letters we wrote are returned to us) can take us back into a forgotten age and illuminate some aspect of the present or remind us of some forgotten aspect of experience. When I look back as far as the little diaries I wrote at seven or eight I do have a frisson of recognition which connects me to my experience – and to those people I mention in the pages (see Journal Prompt: Looking at old writing, p.88).

One client, Fiona, told me of her plan to use the 'no man's land' between Christmas and New Year to re-read her journal of the previous year. She wanted to look for the themes of the year, the achievements and the uncompleted tasks; all these help her to look forward and begin the New Year with a stronger sense of where, and even who, she is.

Journal Prompt: Beginning

What do you feel as you contemplate the page? Ask yourself:

Am I… excited? daunted? overawed? itching to begin? paralysed?

Complete the following:

When I look at this blank page I want to…

When I look at this blank page I feel…

Journal Prompt: The door

Imagine there is a closed door in front of you. Describe the door, what it looks like, feels like, what kind of handle or latch it has.

When you are ready, imagine you take a step forward and open the door ready to step through. What do you find on the other side?

Journal Prompt: What's really going on…

What's really going on for me right now?

Journal Prompt: What do you feel now?

1. Describe the physical sensations in your body as if doing a full body scan. What is your relationship to your body now?
2. What emotions do you feel?
3. What are your thoughts?

Journal Prompt: Looking at a picture

Describe what you can see, follow the connections and memories that arise in what you write so that they lead you beyond the photograph frame.

Who is there?

Who is not there?

Who is behind the camera?

Where is this place?

Have you been there?

What does it say to you now?

Journal Prompt: Looking at old writing

Find your earliest written diaries/letters.

Who do you recognize in the pages? What aspects of yourself are there?

What do you understand now that you didn't then?

CHAPTER 4

Lists

Everyone makes lists. Even people who say 'I never write' write lists. Beginning with lists is a way of engaging reluctant or self-professed non-writers. Making lists is a structured, contained and concrete activity; it can be the first step in writing coherent prose, or poetry. Lists can help manage the chaos of life; they are a way of organizing and prioritizing information. Making lists can structure activity or acknowledge achievement.

This makes them an ideal introduction to structured therapeutic journal writing. They can be short enough to be manageable for people suffering from debilitating conditions like depression or for people on the edge of recovery. The first thing on a list of achievements for a seriously depressed person might be: 'Got out of bed'.

Lists are good for focusing and seeing what the priorities are. Sometimes lists are preludes to more extended exploration (see Chapters 3 and 12), at other times the list itself is the therapeutic intervention (Chapter 11). List-writing provides a manageable task for most people and can be adapted to individual needs. Small lists are particularly appropriate for those who are less literate, dyslexic or second language speakers whose language is still at the noun phrase stage of complexity. The familiarity of the list form is reassuring, its brevity and conciseness is unthreatening.

Different kinds of list

'To do' lists

These can be micro lists such as 'what I have to do tomorrow' or 'people I need to contact'. Below are some examples of former clients who used 'to do' lists.

Using a 'to do' list to regain control: John

John was struggling to keep track of all his appointments (medical, social services, social) and he was really confused and scared of missing something which could mean the loss of benefits or necessary care. This created more self-doubt and even less ability to cope. In order to help him re-gain control of his life he followed the steps below:

1. Buy a diary/planner for recording appointments.

2. Buy a notebook.

3. Each evening write a list in the notebook of what was happening the following day together with the addresses and phone numbers of the appointment places.

The two-book process was important because it allowed him to reinforce the information he had, create a structured task and contain his self-doubt and confusion. This technique resulted in him missing far fewer appointments and feeling less overwhelmed.

An accumulation of short lists allows for recognition of patterns of activity and behaviour; this in turn can lead to change.

Using a 'to do' list to prioritize and manage time: Jill

Jill had a career as a busy professional in television production but now she was, in her own words, 'a stay-at-home mum'. She could not work out why she never seemed to have enough time for all the things that seemed to need to be done. Initially, making a list before bedtime allowed her to make sure she would not forget any of the next day's tasks. Subsequently, it also served to show her that, whilst her life was no longer high profile in one sense, it was very full of things she had to do. She could then start to think about prioritizing.

A typical example of one of Jill's 'A List Before Bedtime':

Laura's gym kit.

Fairy cakes for Tuesday.

Charlie to vet – shots.

Waitrose (shopping list).

Bank.

Ring Margaret, Sue, Caroline re lunch Thursday.

Collect Laura from Emma's 6 pm.

Library books.

Nick's jacket.

Standing items – cleaning, tidying, cleaning, cooking, washing.

A month of 'A List Before Bedtime' enabled her to get an overview of where her time went. This helped her to look at whether there could be a different way of structuring things and even whether everything on the list was necessary. After reflection she re-organized her activity to give her more time for herself.

This made her feel she had the capacity to embrace the unexpected, something which had previously induced feelings of being overwhelmed and inadequate. She designated a couple of days in each month for going to the bank and shopping rather than 'whenever I think about it' which had led to her feeling quite harassed. This cut down the amount of time she spent travelling into town. She explored whether washing was always there and whether she really needed to do some every day (she didn't – Nick had enough shirts to last a week, her daughter had plenty of clothes 'and if her yellow skirt isn't clean she can wear her red one').

After she had developed her list-making habit Jill's feedback was 'One of the best things about keeping lists is ticking things off, seeing that things are done. It makes me feel more organized and capable. Also, the standing items, like the cleaning remind me that there are things which are just there and I don't need to feel guilty about never being able to tick them off.'

This technique could be equally useful for students or busy professionals who fear forgetting something, being unable to achieve their goals or not meeting their targets.

Other micro lists which help with organization but which can also have wider applications include:

- Shopping lists.
- Birthday lists.

- Reward lists (When I finish this book I'll… Get my hair cut; Tidy and polish my desk; Meet friends for lunch; Walk for a whole day).
- Review lists (Things I still haven't finished).
- Christmas card lists.

Then there are macro lists:

- What do I have to do in my life?
- Things I need to do before I'm 50/60/70.
- Project management lists.
- Things to do when moving house.
- Lists of ongoing or future projects, plans and activity.

When things are on a list they seem more manageable because they can be seen in context with other things.

Lists of roles

Everyone plays many roles during a lifetime; and there are times when these roles conflict with each other, leading to dissatisfaction or even pain. These different roles can be called upon to help, support and challenge each other (see Chapter 11). Listing the different external roles can be a way of getting to know them and beginning to integrate them which can have great therapeutic benefit.

Asking members of any therapeutic journal group to list the roles they perform will result in individuals who quickly reach 17 or more; most people get to 10 without pause. After doing the following exercise one group member said 'I didn't know I was so big' (see Journal Prompt: List of roles, p.102).

The list of 100 (Adams 1990)

The list of 100 is the list making journal technique with the most therapeutic potential. A hundred is a magic number in lists for both process and content. It is also statistically easy to analyse the results.

People may find the idea of writing 100 items on a list daunting, but in fact the rules make it simple:

- **Repeat:** you can repeat things as often as you need to, the same things will occur several times and they should be noted as they arise. If you get stuck keep repeating until you are ready to move on.

- **Don't censor:** write down whatever comes to mind – you can evaluate it later.

- **Don't hesitate:** keep writing, try not to 'think' about things or to be distracted with deciding whether they are 'true'.

- **Repeat** whenever your thoughts repeat.

- **Repeat** whenever you are stuck.

The second part of the exercise is to analyse the list by dividing it into categories. There is always one category for Miscellaneous; the categories may be bigger or smaller than anticipated and therein lies some of the possibility for insight and growth.

The list of 100 is where the unconscious mind is invited to appear in list making and where people can make important discoveries about themselves. When introducing this technique to other people, in a group or individual setting, providing them with a pre-numbered sheet with the numbers 1–100 takes away some of the anxiety. Removing the distraction of remembering to keep numbering points as they are written allows the less cognitive process to develop more strongly.

Lists of 100 get below the surface and socially constructed self to tell us what else is going on. Some people discover that the cause of their anger (100 things I'm angry about…) is not what they had thought, or at least not where they were directing it; other people re-discover their respect and liking for themselves or others through this process:

- 100 things I like/value about myself.

- 100 things I like/value about my mother.

- 100 things I don't like.

Within a list of 100 there is naturally a movement from the more concrete to the more abstract. This exercise takes less time than people think – about 25–30 minutes for the initial list and then as much time as needed for the taxonomy and reflection. As a technique for planning and time management the list of 100 can help to prioritize, set actions and intentions. For example:

- 100 things I want to change.

- 100 things I want to do.

Using a list of 100 to determine what you want: Linda

Linda was vaguely dissatisfied with her life but not sure what she wanted to do about it or why she felt like this.
    She wrote:

100 things I want to do

I want to…

1. walk in the park

2. live in a house

3. learn Italian

4. grow herbs

5. get a new job

6. use my degree

7. travel

8. visit Rome

9. be happy

10. get a new job

11. travel

12. live in a house with a garden

13. live alone

14. live abroad

15. move

16. keep moving

17. move on

And so on.

If you look at the example, you can see patterns beginning to emerge in Linda's list. She began with very concrete aspirations – some she could do there and then, while others were obviously a longer-term plan. When she analysed the list, things to do with travel occurred in over 40 per cent of her items. This, combined with a desire for work-related change, directed her to looking for jobs abroad where she could use her degree in Modern Languages. She also decided that the house with a garden could wait – what the list told her was that she was tired of flat-sharing and wanted more independence and space.

Using a list of 100 things to reveal the unconscious: Pete

Pete, a man in his forties, wrote 'A list of 100 things I think about'... He found, buried at number 85, the item:

85. my sister

They had been taken into care years before as children and had lost touch. Although he had not consciously thought of her for many years she surfaced in his list. He said he was surprised to find her popping up now but as a result he was determined to find out what had happened to her. He started to think about some of the other experiences he had buried in his memory. Following this he began to process them and re-construct the narrative of his life.

Clusters

Clusters, also known as 'mind maps' or 'spidergrams', have been used for centuries as aides memoire or planning tools. The psychologist Tony Buzan (2006) developed mind maps as a learning tool for students in the 1960s. Later they were adopted by the business world for project management.

If lists are ways of writing things in a short space of time and paper, clusters take this process of discovery further. They are particularly useful when someone is feeling overwhelmed as they capture a lot of information quickly and visually. They are simply another kind of list and demonstrate that lists do not have to be linear; lists can spread sideways.

It is thought that some people find that a linear list is not a particularly helpful organizational tool for them; their minds want to capture things in a more global way. Conversely, other people are disturbed by the idea of a cluster as they find it rather anarchic and chaotic to sprawl everything anywhere on the paper. For the latter, a gentle and contained introduction to clusters is necessary so that they ultimately find the technique quite liberating.

Some therapists 'mind map' their clients to remember facts about their lives and stories which can be quickly referred to before sessions and become a useful aide memoire. Genograms are a kind of mind map showing the relationships between people and siting someone in the centre of their life and networks, visually depicting connectedness and isolation. Family trees are a kind of list locating people in their heritage and lineage.

Clusters also allow people to let their artistic sides loose and discover their creativity when using coloured pens, different shapes for bubbles, size and shape of script. A cluster can be a work of art (see Journal Prompt: Create a cluster, p.102).

Clusters are very effective for professional planning – whether it is a work project, an essay or a thesis. They are also a very useful time management tool that can allow people to see exactly what needs to be done. They can be used for overcoming writer's block – at least the kind of writer's block which is a surfeit of things to say or ways to say them rather than a blank emptiness.

Writing a continuous piece about a cluster can synthesize and integrate what you can see. The stream of consciousness freedom of the cluster can be cathartic or organizational and it produces the opportunity to determine future action. A cluster shopping list is a way of remembering not just what you need to buy but also why you want it – something which can elude you when you get to the supermarket.

Using a cluster to help to regain a sense of balance: Julie

Julie was struggling with her aging mother's care. She felt it took up a lot of her time and energy and she was beginning to resent it and feel somewhat unappreciated. After she did the cluster shown in Figure 4.1 she wrote:

> This helps me to regain a sense of balance I all this. I had lost sight of my mother as a person with experiences and history and a past relationship with her. I remember her in my childhood – home-made lemonade and a strong sense of being protected. Her widowhood has been hard and the loneliness has become entrenched – how

could it not. I don't need her to show her gratitude, CARE is the keyword – her care for me when I was young, my care for her now and CARE is getting lost in DUTY.

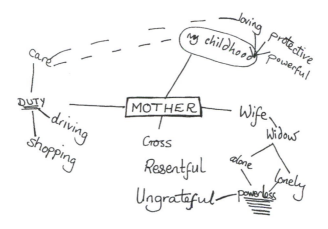

Figure 4.1: Julie's 'mother' cluster

List poems

The rhythm of list poems provides a kind of containment. List poems are created by repeating the same sentence stem/line opening or by taking two contrasting ideas repeated on alternate lines. List poems emulate a familiar rocking rhythm. They can hold ambivalence and ambiguity such as likes and dislikes about the same thing, contrasting opinions or viewpoints. This can also help people to make decisions and move from the paralysis of an ambivalent state.

Using list poems to weigh decisions: Kay

Kay was trying to decide whether to move to the country after years in the city:

Going means walking in fresh air.
    Staying means waking under neon light.

Going is hearing birds, feeling wind, crossing moors on strong legs.
    Staying is the ache of joints on pavements and the sound of traffic passing by.

Going is the freedom of time and knowledge of the self.
 Staying is theatre and concerts and meals out and people.

Going is new knowledge of self and time and place.
 Staying is sure and known and unremarkable.

Going is the excitement of the new.
 Staying is the satisfaction of the known.

Going requires effort and energy and momentum.
 Staying means more of the same and more of the same.

If I stay I'll never know.
 If I go I'll know.

The two worlds she needed to choose between were clearly evoked for her, as were the parts of the self that each one would satisfy. This did not make the choice for her but it did give her more of a basis for making her choice.

Acrostics and AlphaPoems (Adams 1990, 2006)

An acrostic is where the letters of a name or a word are written vertically down the page and each letter begins a line. In the example below, Grace, a grandmother, is making some comment about how her granddaughter, Aline, is growing up, but the acrostic also contains her feeling about how the world is changing:

A *beautiful child you were,*
Loving and giving to all.
I *adored your funny little ways.*
Now you're telling me
Extraordinary tales.

Acrostics are good for entering and engaging with any issues which people are dealing with in their own personal development and can also be used in practice as practical help (see p.200).

Angel cards are small cards which feature a word and an illustration, and can be used to help inspire ideas for acrostics. Words might be, for example, 'Balance', 'Humour' or 'Appreciation'.

A person is invited to pick an angel card at random and when they do so, they often find that it focuses their attention in useful ways.

After her hip replacement Ellie picked the word 'Balance' out of a bowl of angel cards and wrote:

> **B**right green leaves cover the trees
> **A**s she begins to walk along the path
> **L**egs support her again
> **A**fter months of pain
> **N**ewborn experience awaits
> **C**limbing upwards towards
> **E**xpanding horizons

Feedback: When I read this the uncertain rhythm feels like me on my shaky legs, striving to find recovery and balance again, but uncertain like a child. If I change the pronouns it feels more personal and somehow stronger:

> **B**right green leaves cover the trees
> **A**s I begin to walk along my path
> **L**egs support me again
> **A**fter months of pain
> **N**ewborn, experience awaits me
> **C**limbing upwards towards
> **E**xpanding horizons.

Feedback: When I read this version I begin to feel more hopeful – 'Climbing' is a good, strong word and I'm walking my path again.

Acrostics are useful for people who do not want to write much or who are reluctant writers, people who struggle to focus or people who have poor confidence in writing. Children and young people, especially adolescents, are particularly attracted to them. Acrostics based on people's names can make tributes to people or suitable memento mori to show how you feel. They can also become a tool for thinking about someone you are struggling with.

Alesha had been picked on by her classmate Jessie for long enough:

Just you wait
Evil fighting girl
Sometime I'll find you,
Show what you've done to me, but
I won't be frightened no more –
Everyone will know it's you, not me.

Afterwards she said:

> Writing it down made me feel a bit more in control. I don't
> want to fight but I don't want to hide now either. Jessie's just
> a girl like me.

AlphaPoems are extensions of acrostics just as lists of 100 are of lists.
AlphaPoems take the whole alphabet vertically (Adams 1990, 2006).
These can be done in groups as collaborative poem-making exercises
or by individuals working with any particular issue. The alphabet has a
comforting sound, a rhythm which takes us back to early childhood and
the familiarity seems to produce a deeper kind of flow.

The letter 'X' is a wild card – any word beginning phonetically x (ex
or even acce – as in the example) can be used.

Claire was dealing with the transition of her son leaving home and
taking his gap year abroad. She wrote the following AlphaPoem about
it:

Alone here and quiet,
But where have you gone,
Child of mine?
Distant now,
Eating strange food.
Flown,
Grown.
'Home is where the heart is'
I remember someone said;
Just in case we want to
Kaleidoscope back through time –
Look, how I've spread the
Memories here,
Note, how each

One is a family
Photograph not yet in an album,
Quaintly recording times I still
Remember from your growing years:
Sitting on my lap, arms reaching for my face,
Then suddenly taller than me,
Under the oaks at grandma's house.
Viewing your history like this,
Wondering at how it flashed past, I
Xcept and celebrate that I gave
You the courage to leave your comfort
Zone and fly.

Feedback: Yes, I'm sad and finding it strange to be on my own I miss him, of course I do, but I know that it's because I've been an OK mum that he can do this and have these new experiences.

Journal Prompt: List of roles

Write a list of all the roles you play/have played in your life. Write a sentence to describe the kind of person each of them is. For example:

Jill's roles:

Mother Jill is always on the go, never getting things finished.

Friend Jill is reliable and wants to be available – she also knows how to have a good time!

Wife Jill is attentive and there, but she can feel a bit unappreciated.

Daughter Jill is too busy to visit her mother as often as her mother would like but she is good at telephoning.

Sister Jill wishes her sister would do more about her mother.

TV producer Jill is organized, capable and efficient. She never misses deadlines.

Mum-at-the-school-gates Jill has her eyes open all the time to make connections and see how it's done.

Journal Prompt: Create a cluster

Put the chosen word/topic/issue/person in the middle of the page and free associate around it. Write down anything which comes to mind using a word or a short phrase to denote each idea or item. Begin to connect things with links, make groups. Include everything however disconnected it may feel.

CHAPTER 5

———•◆•———

Steppingstones

Steppingstones allow us to connect quickly to the course of our lives. The salient points of a particular narrative thread of our lives can be listed very quickly in Steppingstones. Progoff says: 'The Steppingstones are the significant points of movement along the road of an individual's life' (Progoff 1975, p.102). He calls them 'meaningful markings'. They provide a way of discovering different narrative threads and strands of meaning across the life course.

Each set of Steppingstones is unique to the individual, and to the place and feeling of the time of writing. The traditional exercise is where we let our minds wander over the experience of our lives, letting various memories arise and noting them down with just a word or phrase. Progoff suggests beginning with the first external event of our lives: 'I was born'.

This places you at the beginning of your experience and you can then follow it with the other markers that come to mind. The point is not to list every life event but to notice what seems significant from the perspective at the time of writing (see also Journal Prompt: The Steppingstones method, pp.109–10).

Sue wrote:

I was born.
I went to school.
* *Grandad died.*
I went to college.
I got my first job.
I married.
I had my son.
I got divorced.

This is one set of Steppingstones, but there are other themes. Almost anything can provide a theme for a Steppingstones exercise such as different groups of people who touch our lives:

- Authority figures.

- Family.

- Close friends.

- Lovers.

Or particular kinds of event:

- Birthdays.

- Moves/re-locations.

- Life transitions.

Steppingstones can also come from more abstract topics such as feelings or values. Each element in a set of Steppingstones has the power to connect to a different point in life. For each one a different set of reflections occurs which suggests possibilities for more detailed exploration or further connections. Different themes provide different opportunities; the same theme addressed at different times will produce different results. The listing of the Steppingstones is an interesting and useful exercise (it has the particular benefit of brevity in busy lives) but it is merely the first step in a deeper investigation.

Steppingstones can point to the passage across the choppy and sometimes dangerous waters of life; we can see them and use them to navigate a way through. They are also the precarious supports we balance on as we make our way across, sometimes just under the surface, sometimes safely and clearly out of the water. This can depend as much

STEPPINGSTONES   105

on the level of floodwater in our present as on the moment of the event when it occurred.

Each set of Steppingstones provides a different thread pulling through the fabric of our lives; they illuminate different patterns and meanings.

Different sets of Steppingstones

Crossroads

Penelope Lively's *Making it Up* (2005) is a collection of short stories based on the 'what if…' of her life. She looks at particular crossroads and imagines what would have happened if she had made different choices at salient points of her life. The crossroads include other jobs, other partners and perhaps most dramatically, not going to university but being a pregnant teenager. She finds rich material for her fiction in the roads not taken (see also Journal Prompt: Crossroads, p.110).

<u>Using Steppingstones to think about decisions taken: Sue</u>

Sue discovered that the course she had followed was not such a second best after all and that many of the outcomes would have been the same anyway. She wrote:

It was a time when the choice was given to me on a plate – I could go to university and do my degree or I could stay at home and begin to train in the local hospital. If I went away I'd have to leave Dennis, I'd have to leave my first serious boyfriend, my bedroom with the pink walls, my parents who protected and looked after their only daughter. In the end I couldn't do it. We didn't go to college in our family, not even the boys. I've often wondered what would have happened if I'd gone to Sheffield – would I have stayed with Dennis? We split up anyway six months later. I went to live in the nurse's home and hardly ever went back home for tea.

Angela introduced me to Martin who she met at uni and who came to the hospital for his training – it all might have happened any way. The girl who didn't go to Sheffield still left home and got married and had a career. Perhaps she wasn't ready when the first time was offered – I could do my degree next year as a mature student anyway – I think I will because It's the opportunity I turned down before and always wondered…

The quote below by Progroff is instructive:

> To be able to reenter the intersection of past periods of our lives gives us access to the unlived possibilities of our existence which the future may still give us an opportunity to fulfill, albeit in a different form. (Progoff 1975, p.129)

Landscape Steppingstones

We inhabit different landscapes during our lives. There are places which have some emotional significance and places which have been there for so long that they seem part of an 'internal psychogeography'. Some landscapes have personal landmarks known only to an individual. These private landmarks include things like the site of a first kiss, or the place where an event that exists in an individual's memory occurred. Other places may have made an impact because of their more public significance. These are the internal and external landmarks in the landscapes of our lives. Some of these will be our own 'Blue Remembered Hills' (Housman 1994), others will be shared by many.

The physical landscapes of our lives shape our experience; bigger and smaller landscapes, the intimate geography, the psychogeography, all contribute to making us who we are. It follows that writing about them can increase our understanding of who we are and where we come from. The child who writes her address at the front of her book adding, after street, town and county, her country, continent, the world, the universe, is trying to locate herself in the bigger picture and find her place in the world.

On our way to our regular summer holiday destination I knew we were almost there when we passed the house with the big doll's house in the garden. Re-visiting the area after 30 years I was disorientated to find the doll's house no longer there – how would I know how far there was still to go? In my internal landscape it will remain a landmark (see also Journal Prompt: Landscapes, p.111).

At one workshop I attended, facilitator Julie Ward asked us to describe a tree that we remembered. I had difficulty narrowing down to only one and almost without thinking came up with a list of *Tree Steppingstones*:

The willow tree in the garden of Satis House.
The horse chestnut at Home Farm.
The fallen tree at Rigg Bay.
The 3 pines at the Gebbie house.
The urban cherry tree in Forest Drive East.
The oaks outside my window as I sit here and write.

A vast tree, the horse chestnut at the farm. Its lowest branch, almost down to the grass under its own weight, slight movement up and down. It could support all the children in a row, riding it like a horse. I can feel the stretch of my thighs as I tried to stay on it, the rough-smooth crevices of the bark on my bare child legs. Pigeons flocked it with mournful calls which touch my heart even now and evoke those summer holidays, year after year of sunshine, companions, and complex feelings.

When I read this I am transported to the sights, sounds and feelings of childhood summer holidays. The horse chestnut became a symbol of it all somehow and I want to explore it again.

Each of these trees offers me entry to a different part of my life and the emotions and events of that period. Each one triggers a series of images and feelings and memories and makes them available to me again. They are some of my 'Blue Remembered Hills'. *Hill Steppingstones* is another list...

Sometimes the significance of a particular place in the development of personality or character only becomes known when written about retrospectively. Sarah's evocation of a particular time and place below allowed her to see how the security provided by that relationship and experience formed her adult character, how she became a woman who was unafraid to take risks and move beyond her comfort zone:

Daddy's shoulders at the beach at Point Lookout

I'm at Point Lookout on a hot summer's day. The warmth of the sun has always felt like a blanket enveloping me in a loving embrace. And the feel of the sand, the smell of the salt air and the sounds of the ocean as the waves break are all my friends. The ocean coming in and going out...

Daddy would plant the base of the umbrella into the sand with back-and-forth motions – first in a north/south direction and then in an east/west direction until it was deep enough to support the umbrella so firmly that it never blew away or over if a strong wind came up. Then we'd put down towels right up against the umbrella pole and put the thermos (with Daddy's famous pink lemonade) and the lunch on the towels and cover them with more towels. We'd strip off our clothes, hang them on the underside spokes of the umbrella and run as fast as we could toward the water…giggling in excitement.

Once in the water, Daddy would lift us onto his shoulders by ducking down into the water and reaching up to take our hands while we climbed on board. From on top of his shoulders, I had the same view of the beach and the ocean that Daddy had – I could see the colours on the tops of the beach umbrellas and see the approaching waves more clearly. Then Daddy would toss me into the ocean…teaching me the fearlessness that I carry to this day and making risk-taking as natural as falling off a log.

When I read this I feel:

grateful to Daddy

sad that those times are gone

amazed to realize that this simple pleasure helped and taught me to be a risk taker.

People as Steppingstones

Distinct categories of people and relationships can form sets of steppingstones to pull different threads in our lives. These might include:

- Significant relationships – lovers, friends, colleagues.

- People in authority (this could lead to the faces of our Inner Critic, that powerful internal voice which seems bent on cutting us down to size, keeping us in our place, sabotaging our desires; (see Wolton 2006).

- Heroes/mentors/influences.

Houses and homes

This can be done pictorially (see Chapter 11) by drawing all the houses you have lived in as if they were next to each other in the same street so you can visit each one in turn. Later write a description of each of them as if re-visiting them.

Books or music

This is the idea on which the long-running radio programme *Desert Island Discs* is based. A guest chooses eight pieces of music that have significance and allow them to sum up their lives in a 45-minute programme. Music often represents different stages and events in our development and can remain evocative and imbued with emotional experience (see Journal Prompt: Music Steppingstones [Desert Island Discs], p.111).

Journal Prompt: The Steppingstones method

Step 1

Notice the Steppingstones as they occur to you (which may or may not be the chronological order in which they happened).

Note each one with just a word or a brief phrase to identify it.

[Do not allow yourself to dwell too long – sometimes people are seduced into a more detailed investigation of the event and find themselves already at this stage writing a sentence or a paragraph or more – this stage results in simply a list, not a piece of continuous prose.]

Stop when you have listed about eight, certainly not more than 10 or 12 [this constraint allows for selectivity and for the ones of greatest significance to step forward, it also allows particular threads to emerge.]

Step 2

Number the Steppingstones in chronological order.

Read them aloud in chronological order (whether in a group or on your own – the purpose of reading them is for you to hear the flow of your experience).

[If time is short, simply note down any general reflections about the list and set it aside for another time.]

Step 3

Choose one of the Steppingstones which you would like to investigate more closely, perhaps one which seems to look larger, have more substance than others at this time. This now offers the opportunity for a deeper reflection.

Begin by locating the event in the period of your life to which it belongs:

'It was a time when I...'

Gradually focus down to describe the Steppingstone in as much detail as is available to you, include the external and internal events, the changes and people, your values and desires at the time.

Journal Prompt: Crossroads

Allow your mind to wander back over your life.

Notice any times when you:

(a) made a decision

or

(b) had a decision made for you (this can be even more revealing about the relationships and people in your life)

or

(c) a time when something happened over which you had no control that determined 'what happened next' or changed something in your life.

List these crossroads or intersections, these points when things could have gone another way, either by your choice or despite your will. Notice the ambiguities.

Choose one of the crossroad Steppingstones and begin to write:

'It was a time when...'

Describe the circumstances in which this event happened and go on to explore what might have happened if the decision or event had had a different outcome.

Journal Prompt: Landscapes

Let your mind wander over the places you've been, small and large, urban and rural, passing through or setting roots, big vistas or intimate spaces. Notice the public and private landmarks that show up in your landscape. List the places in the order they come to mind with just a name or a phrase to identify them.

Journal Prompt: Music Steppingstones (Desert Island Discs)

Begin with the first piece of music that you can remember.

What are the memories and feelings which you associate with this now?

——————•◆•◆•◆•——————

CHAPTER 6

Description and Deeper

Description is a style of writing which both focuses on and preserves memories of events, feelings, people or places in a way that enables the undoing of the oblivion of time. It is also a way of developing and discovering a creative voice. However, it is not the only element in personal writing, and is not present in all journal writing. Describing an experience, a feeling, a landscape or a person means paying attention and attempting to capture it. This is one way of observing the world.

To describe something is to connect more deeply with it than merely to report it. But it is important to remind people that: 'whatever you describe, you are also describing your perception and experience of it – other people will have their own views.'

One woman who wrote a character sketch of her admired father showed it to her brother who did not recognize the person she described at all. In a more dramatic case another woman who showed her description of her abusive father to her siblings changed her relationship with them for many years.

Different people will retain different memories of people and events; their descriptions will never be identical. Sometimes they have accepted others' descriptions without question and only when they come to write their own do they discover that their perceptions and experiences are really different. Family myths and stories can often grow into an orthodoxy in which challenge is not permitted. Finding and recording authentic experience is powerfully therapeutic but can be painful too.

Detail captures experience when using description as a therapeutic journal writing tool, making it vivid and powerful again when re-read. This leads to further insights which are recorded in the feedback loop (see p.34–37).

By making such evocative transcripts of experience we confer a greater importance to our own existence. Tristine Rainer says: 'As a woman I feel that my power to describe my life is a gesture against powerlessness' (Rainer 1977, p.61). This is true not only of women, of course, but of anyone or any group which feels disempowered or oppressed. When we read diarists of the past, description of the details of their lives enables us to enter into their worlds and experiences; description brings the past, and the deceased, alive.

Captured moments

Description is a way of capturing particular memories for posterity, for future reflections or even for future generations. 'Captured moments' (Adams 1990) is a particular technique for re-entering a memory and examining it in the light of present reality. It can be used to find and fix, like a photograph, experiences in the recent past (today, the last week, the last month) or from the more distant past. People have found that writing captured moments from years ago can illuminate some aspect of the present or recover some aspect of themselves with which they had lost contact. Describing something through our sensory experience, the 'felt experience', can capture an evocative truth (see Journal Prompt: Captured moment, p.123). Novelist Richard Ford stresses the importance of recording sensation:

> My novelist's version of sensation, of being up against the world, is to keep my nose pressed similarly up to the palpable, mutable, visible, audible, smellable and for the most part disorderly world, flooded as it is with exquisite, intractable, irresistible, details. (*The Guardian* 2009)

Often a captured moment will provide an intense experience of recollection; sometimes this can be quite unexpected. The emotion of the memory, the feeling tone, which appears in the writing is not necessarily the one you might have anticipated or thought you held in mind.

Jasmine wrote about the first time she saw her future husband:

> The knock on the door startles me, I'm dozing in the couch, the rough weave of the Mexican blanket across my knees. The radio burbles to my left, the incense burns sweetly. This is how I like my evenings – peaceful, quiet, uninterrupted. The knock on the door startles me. I'm not expecting anyone and I feel a little irritated at the interruption. Perhaps they'll go away.
>
> 'Come in' I call, perhaps rather quietly, but they don't hear me, the knock comes again, louder, demanding. I don't recognize it, as if you can recognize a knock on the door. I'm irritated, disturbed, unsure. I throw the blanket back and unsteadily, because I'm sleepy, cross the carpet in bare feet to the door. Cautiously? Anxiously? I open the door, the handle is metal, is cold, I pull it down and the latch clicks. Sarah and a man I don't recognize are standing there, expectantly. I wonder if I've forgotten something.
>
> When I read this I'm surprised at how vividly I can recall the peaceful existence I had before I met Matt, even though it's years ago now. I was quite content in my little room, I'd forgotten that. Actually life didn't begin when I met him – it just changed. When was the last time I had a peaceful evening under a blanket on the couch? Maybe that's what I need.

Captured moments in the moment

Every time I describe the view from my window it grounds me, it locates me where I am in time and space which can be very useful when trying to re-gain focus. And every time I describe it it's different:

7.30 am

The sky is a uniform grey, bright, pale, without variation, like the paper in which the foreground is printed. The trees are motionless, larch, silver birch, two kinds of pine and one stunted oak. Their trunks all different in colour and texture. Bedraggled sheep nibble their way up the slope, heads down, legs following the nose. They are all stomach. The alert sentry call of the nuthatch signals danger, the thrum of the generator, somewhere between a hum and a whine and the house settling into its morning self. I'm peaceful here at my desk looking out.

12.00 pm

Sky all movement and light, clouds pass behind the trees. A walker crosses the slope, shoulders hunched against the wind, sheep chew and stare. A blackbird or some other songbird calls up and down and round a scale. The trees wave, the larch is a particular dancer. There is energy in the scene now, and my own energy and appetite for work has grown through the morning.

When I compare the paragraphs I am aware of how my energy has grown and I am more engaged in what I am doing with no desire to pull away just yet.

Every time a colleague sends me an e-mail snapshot of the view from her window I am connected to her across time and climate zones.

Travel journals

People often say that they keep a diary/journal on holiday or when travelling, but not during the rest of the year or in normal life. Travel writing lends itself to description; the best travel writing is not just an evocation of place but a reflection of a person at a time and in a place.

My mother kept a diary of daily activity and mostly impersonal events, but she also kept travel diaries which are much more evocative (especially when they record things my own journals missed). Her attention to detail and her curiosity about her environment fills the pages of her travel diaries with historical and natural detail. I realize now that her interest was very much in the environment rather than in the people. I bring my own experience to the reading of it and the frustration about the lack of personal introspection is entirely mine. When I look closely there is a lot of implicit personal feeling.

From my mother's diary:

Thursday 5th of April 1990

The Merced river raced and tumbled over its rocky bed, looking very clear and cold. After lunch we set off up the track to Mirror Lake but when we were almost there, the clouds gathered over the great cliffs, lightning flashed and the heavens opened. Robin was in his pushchair and none of us was clad for heavy rain! By tremendous luck, a Park ranger (Colin Campbell) was cruising by in his large car, and picked us up just as the sleet started. We owed our luck to Robin – I don't suppose he would have stopped for adults.

My reflection (2009):

This evokes the experience entirely for me. I can feel the relentless rain on the back of my neck and the heft of the pushchair filled with a toddler's weight. I can almost imagine the smell of the ranger's car full of damp clothes. And it makes me feel connected to my mother probably in a way I wasn't in my prickly twenties.

<u>Using a joint travel diary therapeutically: Joan and Patrick</u>

Kim and Patrick always kept a joint travel diary when they went on holiday – often Patrick wrote the text and Joan illustrated it with sketches or things she collected en route. They were able to look back together over their travels and when they could no longer go travelling the journals would stand as records for them, and later for their children, of a significant part of their life together. As Patrick began the descent into Alzheimer's the journals remained a place where Joan and he connected, long after the present became fragmented. Joan's therapist encouraged her to keep reading the journals to Patrick and reminding him of the travels they had shared. For Joan this was deeply therapeutic and she believed it was for Patrick too.

Working with photographs

Photographs are a useful prompt for all writers. Creative and therapeutic writers use them for inspiration, for honing descriptive powers, for scene setting and character development or for self-discovery and memory recovery (Schneider and Killick 1998; Hunt 2000). All writing teachers have exercises based on photographs.

For therapeutic journal writing, photographs have a particular richness. They offer many opportunities for reflection, deepening insight and another way of developing the relationship with the self. Photographs confront people with visual representations rich in possibility and hidden meaning.

Personal photographs can provide an instant road into the past and begin to unlock memories. Sometimes they don't say anything at first, they refuse to give up their secrets and have to be coaxed – consider the following questions:

- What makes a photograph recognizable on a physical, emotional or intellectual level?

- Why do some photographs open the door to a host of memories, but others seem cut off from known experience, as if they belonged to someone else's life?

Sometimes the question 'Who's missing?' points to the rich material for exploration, the key to unlock the self in experience.

When people are asked to find a photograph of themselves in childhood, they often produce a posed, stiff, school photograph from some time ago, or a faded holiday group. These are the pictures which have come from the family archive, which have survived the different phases of change, moving houses, the disasters, the de-clutterings and the inheritances. Sometimes they come straight from the mantelpiece in a silver frame or have been taken out of family albums (Journal Prompt: Photograph of a younger self, p.124).

> Sharon looked at a school photo of herself, gap-toothed, hair in a ponytail and an obviously hand-knitted cardigan. She wrote:
>
>> She's wearing a hideous, puke green cardigan – it's not even nearly regulation bottle green. Her Nan knitted it but her mother made her wear to school. It was never right and everyone knew it. The other girls pointed and sneered – they wore machine knitted cardigans in sensible colours from British Home Stores or Marks and Spencer's. Karen Hutchinson had a bottle green one from Debenhams (posh eh?). Hand-knitted cardies were unfortunately indestructible and completely humiliating – even wearing braces was not so painful.

> How could a mother do that to a daughter…? How could she not
> know?
>> I made damn sure I never did it to mine – other sins no doubt,
>> they'll tell you, but not that.

Sometimes specific memories can be attached to photographs but
sometimes it seems as if we are seeing the subject for the first time
and feel as if we know little about it. To begin with we stay with the
evidence; what is visible or suggested by the picture.

Writing in this way can help people to re-acquaint themselves with
earlier experiences, the people they were, the lives they lived. Starting
with the concrete and visible evidence:

1. What does s/he want from you?

2. What wisdom/advice can you offer him/her?

This can produce some very moving writing and lead to healing and
reconciliatory experiences.

> Joan, now a 74-year-old widow, looked at the picture in front of her of
> an unsmiling, obviously unhappy, small girl in a coat, clutching a teddy
> bear, a parcel at her feet – it was taken on the day she was evacuated
> during the war.

>> Little Joan, I want you to know that the war will end and you will go
>> home again. I know how frightened you are at this time but it won't
>> always be like this. But it won't ever be the same again but you will
>> survive and grow up. You shouldn't be so afraid, even if it's dark at
>> night.

> Tears came to her eyes as she remembered the little girl's terror at
> being separated from her parents, which was even greater than her fear
> at the sound of the bombs.
> As a result of this exercise, Joan realized that she wanted to write
> about those times and her memories of the war and that turbulent
> period in her own and the world's history. She wanted her grandchildren
> to know about it from her and she wanted to leave something of herself
> to them by doing it.

Working with photographs from different periods of our lives can
connect up threads in our history (they can be Steppingstones, see
Chapter 5) and understand some of the factors and events which formed
us and which make up the continuous narrative of our lives. Photographs

of other people in our lives or ancestry can be similarly enlightening to work with – Victorian relatives in their stiff best clothes show character in their poses. Family groups can remind us of group dynamics and context.

> Steve looked at a happy family group on a beach consisting of himself, his two brothers and his mother, his father was presumably behind the lens. He could not remember the occasion or location. Steve had little recollection of any congenial or happy family occasions such as the one suggested by the photograph. But as he began to write his description of what he could see he began to remember that indeed there had been happy times – but that they were before his father died when he was six – he had not been able to remember them previously. Even though he had seen such photographs on countless occasions he had never felt any connection to them. It was significant to him that his father was not visible in the photograph but was a presence in it all the same.
>
> He went on to work with a photograph of his father and gradually was able to do the work of grieving and loss that he needed.

Writing in the third person, as Steve did, in a narrative or observational way, can gradually begin to open the doors to memory, and connect us to our own past and emotional history. We can then re-enter and inhabit them in a deeper and more personal way.

Photographs of places

> The places where I used to go, but cannot come again. (A.E. Housman 1994)

> Writing about a photograph which evoked a place, Louise wrote the following:

> > The photograph was just lying at the bottom of a drawer. I came across it quite unexpectedly and suddenly I was there. My memories aren't black and white but the black and white photo could have been in colour my memory overlaid it, transformed it so quickly. It became a film.

> > The house has gone but seeing the photo I was there again – I can feel the black metal cat-shaped bootscraper by the door, I expect Gran to open the black front door in her flowery pinny, I can hear

her say 'come in, duck,' and I can smell the beeswax and roasting meat and know what's behind the door.

Feedback: When I read this I feel comforted; although I'm moving house (yet again) there are houses in my memory which I'll have forever.

Photographs can be journal prompts for imagining or remembering a safe place, a sanctuary to hold in our minds.

As part of developing strategies for her anxiety and managing the onset of panic attacks Chris had a photograph of a field with sheep from a previous holiday. By using this as the stimulus for a Captured moment (p.113–115) she created the image of a safe place in her mind which she could call up at the first indication of an imminent panic attack. This soothed her, slowed her breathing and distracted her from her anxiety.

Visual journals

Written journals are one kind and then there are visual or pictorial journals. Artists' notebooks are journals of their creative development in pictures as writers' notebooks are journals of their creative development in words.

In *Drawing from Life* (New 2005) Jennifer New has collected visual journals kept by people from many walks of life, cultures and professions. She says that all visual journals begin with observation and move to reflection. Amongst the examples are maps, drawings, photographs and collages which chart people's lives, vividly and often intimately.

One example is Masayoshi Nagano who drew extremely intricate and detailed maps to depict his morning walks. His daughter-in-law said that this was a way for him to understand his roots more deeply. He continued his practice for a quarter of a century and then destroyed all except one volume; for him their value lay in the process of their making rather than the product.

Art therapists such as Liesl Silverstone (Silverstone 2009) encourage people to do exercises which are visual equivalents of written journal exercises. Collages, sketches, cutting out letters, words or pictures from newspapers or magazines are all techniques for visual or pictorial journals which can be used to therapeutic effect. Combining words and pictures give a different insight into inner process and thinking.

For children and young people visual journals seem a natural way to record their lives and create their own records. Some people's minds more naturally 'see' things pictorially and diagrammatically rather than verbally. Many people will find that a combination of words and pictures takes them to the heart of the matter thus enabling them to make new discoveries and connections.

Circles can have a particular significance; a history of their symbolism exists in various cultures. It is then perhaps not surprising that circles should be used as an art journal device. Psychotherapist and artist Carry Gorney was introduced to them by an art therapist friend. This is her story of the power of drawing circles.

Circles

The Circle Journal, a personal experience

Christmas 2004: Joolz, my art therapist friend, gave me a pristine pack of sparkling gel pens and a new notebook with a Picasso quote on the cover: 'The inner me is necessarily in the canvas because I am the one who makes it.'

'I'm doing circles this year', she said, 'One a day, why don't we both have a go? They're called Mandalas.'

So I did.

Every evening through the long winter I drew and coloured a circle.

Between December 29th and April 4th the colours were cool, mauve and blue, lots of grey, bare stick like patterns, sometimes vivid zigzags cutting across an icy background. My circles were small, constrained, images often radiating from the centre, sometimes spilling over the circumference and trailing down the page.

In my first circle I wrote:

If this was a sand painting the tide would wash over it.

The wind would blow it away.

On New Year's Day we went to Cleethorpes to look at the sea and I drew my circle in the car, whilst clutching a steaming cup of cocoa. I wrote around its rim of orange and blue patterns:

The renewal of cells-the dance of the hormones.

The sound of sleeping, the silence of winter.

The rhythm of our heartbeat.

The sound of the tide in and out.

January 7th: my mauve circle had some green leaves tumbling over it, with red edging and across the top of the page:

Today the wind was blowing; the dark clouds across a pale grey sky.

Trees were swaying and bending their naked branches against the sky.

The mothers clutching their children's hands were bent sideways – whisps of hair blowing wildly whilst passing old ladies holding onto their hats with narrowed eyes.

I was driving to work.

I'm waiting for snowdrops'

Suddenly on April 7th my circles were huge on the page, and painted in bold watercolour stripes and swirls; between April and July they became increasingly vivid, sometimes a mass of green and blue pastels radiating from the middle with yellow edgings, other times flowers were dropped on to the circle, delicate cowslips, a giant pansy leaf, bright blowsy red tulips falling over the page. Little notes were pushed into the pages saying:

Drip drip orange paint on a thick brush.

I'll paint in pink and silver every day.

Drip drip on the face of the sunflower (a huge messy painted orange sunflower filled that page).

In July I started painting the faces of huge daisy shapes; every day another rainbow formalized by silver gold copper tips and edgings on the petals: I have to keep painting the flowers before they go

Later in the year the circles became smaller again, back to the gel pens, constrained, images of rain and grey skies and restriction, sometimes hurried.

The next Christmas arrived; we brought our circles and marked the celebration after work with cake and coffee in the little art room. We opened our books. I gasped at the maze of fiery geometric shapes that were Joolz's. She watched the seasons unfurl as she turned my pages and the light pour onto the page and then slowly recede again as the next winter drew near.

Joolz had not revealed to me that traditionally Mandala work was mainly around geometric patterns and my year of circles burst forth on to the page with a range of loose and random images that came from somewhere within myself.

I know they reflected the seasons, my relationship with the natural world and their affect on my mood. In my circles I saw light and dark, liberty and constraint, sadness and joy, fear and hope.

Mandala in Sanskrit means 'essence' and 'having' or 'containing'. It also translates as 'circle-circumference' or 'completion'. Both derive from the Tibetan term dkyil khor, a concentric diagram having spiritual and ritual significance in both.

I learned that Carl Jung (1995) had become fascinated by circular Mandala images, which are used in meditation practices in Hindu and Buddhist religions. They are found in Christianity under the form of frescos with animal images representing apostles (and the zodiac). Carl Jung saw them as an expression of the unconscious.

I saw that everything, all paths I had been following, all steps I had taken, were leading back to a single point – namely, to the mid-point. It became increasingly plain to me that the Mandala is the centre. It is the exponent of all paths. It is the path to the centre, to individuation.

I knew that in finding the Mandala as an expression of the self I had attained what was for me the ultimate. (Jung 1995, p.228)

Journal Prompt: Captured moment

Choose a particular period of time from which to extract a captured moment – it could be today or your whole life or anything in between.

Close your eyes, think back over the chosen period, notice which memories or moments rise to the surface and call for your attention.

When you are ready, begin to describe the memory in:

  The first person.

  The present tense.

Include as much sensory detail as you can.

Use all the senses: sight, smell, sound, touch, taste.

Notice who else is there or if you are alone or if there is anyone missing.

Journal Prompt: Photograph of a younger self

Find a picture of yourself at some earlier point in you life, preferably childhood.

[If you have no photograph of yourself can you remember ever having seen one – have you got a memory of a photograph which you can work with?

What is it like to have no photographs of yourself in your own past? How do you remember being at school?]

Look at the photograph – begin to describe it:

> When I look at this photograph I see a girl/boy/woman/man who is _____
>
> S/he's wearing _____
>
> S/he looks _____

First describe the physical details of the photograph, the features, the clothes, the scenery/setting, the colours.

What was the weather like?

Then think about the senses – what sounds, smells, textures would have accompanied the photograph?

Then think about the expressions and emotions in the photograph. This can lead us to the feelings and emotions of the period of the photograph.

Gradually move beyond the frame and the visible features to questions like:

> Who else was there?
>
> What was his/her (the younger self) life like at the time?
>
> It was a period when _____

This final prompt can take us back into our experience of ourselves at an earlier stage of our lives.

PART THREE

Less Structured Techniques

CHAPTER 7

——•◆•——

Journal Dialogues

Journal dialogues are conversations between two or more participants. The participants can be almost anyone or anything; they can be people, living or dead or unborn, they can be places, body parts, parts of the self, feelings or activities, the list is endless – wherever there is a question or a curiosity or an openness to allowing ourselves to see what we can learn, there can be a journal dialogue.

Whoever the dialogue participants, the framework is the same (see also Journal Prompt: The dialogue method, p.136). The dialogue begins with a greeting, then a question and continues backwards and forwards between the participants until they are ready to say goodbye. On the page a dialogue looks like the script of a film or play rather than the conversation in a novel (*Women in Love* would be much easier to read if D.H. Lawrence had indicated whether it was Gudrun, Ursula or Hermione speaking).

If a lull in the dialogue occurs the following prompts can move it on:

Is there anything you want to say to me that you haven't said yet?

How can we work together?

Is there anything else you want from me?

What can you teach me?

Prompts like these can also move the dialogue to the next level, to a deeper awareness and understanding which is necessary for healing, growth or integration to occur. They can facilitate change and allow new or unknown material to become conscious.

Progoff calls dialogue 'the realm of interior communication', and sees the 'fundamental sense of dialogue not as a technique but as a *way of relationship*' (Progoff 1975, p.159). Chapters on dialogue occupy nearly half of his book, *At a Journal Workshop*, and is where much of the deeper work of therapeutic journal writing can occur: 'The dialogue relationship is a mutual meeting of persons, each accepting, speaking to, and most important, listening to the other' (Progoff 1975, p.159).

Types of dialogue

Progoff (1975) offers the following categories of dialogue:

- People.

- Works.

- The Body (in which I would include illness/disease/health, medical treatment, addictions).

- Events.

- Society.

- Inner Wisdom.

Kathleen Adams (1990) adds four more categories to his list:

- Emotions/Feelings.

- Material Objects/Possessions.

- Sub-Personalities/Symbols (in which I would include multiple personalities as well as past and future selves here).

- Resistance/Block.

(See also Journal Prompt: Writing a journal dialogue, p.136.)

Traditions of therapeutic dialogue

Therapeutic dialogue has been used and developed over a period of decades by therapists, writers and diarists of all kinds, particularly Gestalt therapists, who commonly use the empty chair technique, which is a dialogue in the room (Clarkson 2004).

Gestalt dialogues are often about re-integrating parts of the self whilst more psychoanalytic practitioners use dialogue to access split-off parts of the self, or have conversations between true self and false self. Therapeutic journal dialogues are simply a written form of this kind of work.

Jeannnie Wright provides a case study 'of one woman's (Jane's) experience of dialogical journal writing which presents a way of finding a "compassionate image" for self-therapy' (Wright 2009). She describes how the complexity and efficacy of Jane's writing developed as she experimented with dialogues and allowed a strongly positive dialogue partner to emerge: 'At first Jane tended to write in descriptive ways, about a favourite teacher or a person she admired and would like to emulate. Gradually, from that novice stage a dialogical form of writing has developed, very much using a maternal, nurturing "compassionate image" to coach and encourage (Gilbert 2005)' (Wright 2009, p.237). In fact, anyone or anything can participate in a journal dialogue.

Two other writers who have developed particular dialogue techniques are Cheryl Moskowitz (1998) and River Wolton (2006). Cheryl Moskowitz's 'The self as source' separates parts of the self and allows them to have a dialogue with each other. This increases acceptance and integration of apparently disparate selves or roles. River Wolton (2006) teaches people to dialogue with their inner critic and begin to make an ally of it which robs it of the power to harm and control.

Practising dialoguing in therapeutic journal writing

I was delighted when training a group of counsellors who all saw dialogues as immediately accessible and useful, though some may have had reservations. Below, I include the response of one course attendee called Doris:

'If anyone heard what was going on in my head, they'd think I was mad.' Doris looked sheepishly at me, looking for reassurance that I didn't think her 'mad' and also looking provocatively to engage my curiosity. I waited. 'Sometimes I even talk to myself', she continued. Again the guarded look with an element of challenge. 'Have you thought of writing these conversations down?' I asked. Her eyes widened – perhaps I were mad (therapist heal thyself?), mocking, or manipulative. Was I trying to catch her out with my question? She needed reassurance and guidance.

This 'listening to' which journal dialogues permit is something that is crucial to both personal development and healing.

When it is introduced, the journal dialogue can seem counter-intuitive and, whilst some people do take to it immediately, many people will find it feels strange and uncomfortable, at least the first time. However, with persistence, and with practice, it becomes an essential and most versatile way of working.

At her first attempt, one client, Julia, said plaintively, 'But I'm just making it up'. She seemed disappointed that another voice hadn't come from somewhere else. Despite Julia's experience, it can seem in dialogues as if another voice has appeared, and that an unknown, possibly unrecognized voice is speaking from somewhere. In this way previously unexpressed thoughts and feelings emerge on the page and other parts of the self, often less familiar selves, make themselves known.

Dialogues can allow a previously silent part of the self to find a voice. When this happens the dialogue seems to write itself. When it is read back people begin to meet their other selves, and to know them, as if for the first time. Often in therapeutic journal work people look over what they've written and say in wonder: 'Where did *that* come from?' In dialogue writing this seems to happen with even greater frequency and power.

One former client called Dan had an initial thought that writing a dialogue between parts of himself was a step towards a 'hearing voices' diagnosis and that a judgemental society would consider it to be indicative of psychosis. In fact, rather than being a form of separation and fragmentation, writing journal dialogues can lead to integration and acceptance.

Both of the individuals mentioned above, Julia and Dan, came to see the possibilities of letting different voices appear in their journals, sometimes disagreeing, sometimes informing, sometimes reaching a fresh understanding. Dan in particular began to relish his dialogue writing. He enjoyed the naming of parts and then letting all of them have their say. In the end he had a sense of sitting back and listening to them and learning from them.

Dialogue writing is a technique that can initially require practice and perseverance, but it can then have surprising results. And perhaps in the end it is not so counter-intuitive – after all, which of us has not had conversations, sometimes incessant, in the privacy of our own head? Journal dialogues are just writing those conversations down and having others.

What are journal dialogues useful for?

Journal dialogues can help to:

- make decisions
- look at unfinished business
- change or modify behaviour
- gain clarity and understanding
- overcome writing blocks
- come to terms with difficult situations
- improve relationships and communication.

Dialogues with people

Suitable dialogue partners can be living or dead, you may or may not still be in contact with them, you may never even have met them but they will be people whose existence mattered to you, however briefly. Sometimes they may be people you have not and will not meet but about whom you are curious or from whom you can learn, such as an admired role model or an idol. You can also dialogue with fictional characters who embody some part of your experience or feelings. The list may include:

- Relatives.
- Ancestors.
- Lovers.
- Friends.
- Colleagues.

There may be an unresolved or incomplete aspect of the relationship or there may be some curiosity or a feeling that something needs to happen or be clarified. Journal dialogues give you an opportunity to have conversations that never happened, can't happen or haven't happened yet.

Dialogue with others: Helen

After her mother died Helen wrote the following dialogue:

Helen: I want to ask you whether you ever really loved me. It's hard to say it but I really want to know. Did you really love me?

Mother: Of course I did. How can you ask me that? You sound as if you doubt it.

Helen: It's just that…no, I didn't always feel that. After I left home you never came to stay with me, you never seemed to want to know what I was doing; you just wanted to talk about yourself and what you were doing.

Mother: Oh Helen, no, it wasn't that I didn't want to know. I was just, well, just busy, I suppose, trying to get used to you not being there, being on my own again. Things started to get very busy in my life too, when you went to university, I met Geoff…

Helen: Yes, that's another thing – first I knew about him was when I came home and he was there, and he stayed; after that he was always there, and you were only interested in him.

Mother: You never liked him and now you sound quite jealous – didn't you want me to be happy?

Helen: Of course I did…oh…

Mother: He's not a bad man you know, and he was good to me after your father died...

Reflecting on what she had written led Helen to re-examine her attitude to her mother and step-father and allowed her subsequently to begin to have a relationship with him after all.

Feedback: When I read this I can see that I was jealous, and we were both self-centred, concerned with our own lives. I think I felt pushed out and I was only 19 and it no longer felt like my home – but I was the one who was leaving, the adjustment was just too quick. Geoff isn't a bad man and we are both grieving now, we've both lost.

In work situations a journal dialogue can help resolve conflict, reach a clearer understanding of something and prepare for difficult or important conversations.

Peter wrote a journal dialogue before an important meeting with his boss. It helped him to find the necessary assertiveness to be heard. Instead of waiting to be criticized he chose to begin:

Peter: Look, I don't suppose you think I've met my targets, do you?

Boss: You suppose right, John, because you haven't.

Peter: I know but...

Boss: Well? What can you say? You haven't met them.

Peter: I know.

Boss: So?

Peter: OK, please don't interrupt me again. I haven't met my targets and I don't want to make excuses but after April they became impossible – my whole department was taken away but the targets didn't change. I wrote business plans, I raised the risk management issues, I pointed out that the job could not be done with the resources I was left with. But no one listened. I even spoke to the board. But no one listened. And I'd like to ask you to listen to what I'm saying.

Boss: I see. Show me those plans again and we'll talk about them.

Feedback: When I read this I recognize how difficult it will be to get him to listen to me – he always interrupts and tries to stamp his authority on the conversation. In the past this has made me lose sight of what I want to say, even doubt my own self, but this time I know what I need to do and where I am. I want to hold on to that.

Dialogue with aspects of the self

Dialogue with the self can help you to reach decisions, make plans, resolve inner conflicts and shift stuckness. It can also help you begin to process and acknowledge things to yourself which you previously had not understood.

> Dan, after his initial resistance to the technique, filled pages of his journal with dialogues between parts of himself. The following is a typical example:
>
> **Risk taker:** How come you always hold me back?
>
> **Cautious self:** What do you mean? I let you drag me into all kinds of situations where we didn't ought to go.
>
> **Risk taker:** What d'you mean 'didn't ought to'? I just want to have some fun and not skulk at home all the time – which is what you'd do if I let you.
>
> **Cautious self:** It's OK for you to want 'fun' as you call it – I'm the one who has to explain things afterwards – like why you were late for work and why you had a hangover so couldn't make your appointment. Don't think I don't get bored being the 'good guy' all the time but someone has to be responsible round here.
>
> **Risk taker:** Just relax. What do you want to do?
>
> **Cautious self:** I want to have fun too but I don't want to go too far – like the time you got threatened by that guy at the club…
>
> **Risk taker:** OK – that was a mistake, I admit it. But at least you stayed around. Thank you – I needed you.
>
> **Feedback:** When I read this I can see the two parts of myself. I realize how they have often kept me in a state of indecision and discomfort as I oscillate between them.

Eventually he began to integrate the different parts of himself as he got to know them better through his journal dialogues. The risk taker and the cautious self began to work together and he began to see that they were both important facets of the self.

Dialogue with the body

Often we are oblivious of the life of the body, the physical self, until it begins to hurt or call attention to itself in uncomfortable ways.

> After twisting her ankle while running, Helen had a dialogue with her body.
>
> **Helen:** How are you feeling today?
>
> **Body:** I'm tired and I ache and it's hard.
>
> **Helen:** Well, you should have seen that extra step and not gone over. Now we're stuck here and have to make the best of it.
>
> **Body:** You feel as if I've let you down, don't you?
>
> **Helen:** Oh, a bit, I'm cross and frustrated and I suppose I'm blaming you.
>
> **Body:** You sound like a baby whose candy's been stolen.
>
> **Helen:** That's a bit how I feel, I feel deprived. Running is important to me. I feel so good when we are out there away from it all and feeling strong and healthy. Mostly you support me and give me so much.
>
> **Body:** It won't be long. We have to be patient though and find a way of staying healthy.
>
> **Helen:** So perhaps a bit of gentle yoga will be good for us, not a deprivation after all.
>
> **Body:** I'll give it a try.
>
> **Helen:** Me too.
>
> **Feedback:** When I read this I am really in touch with my frustration and see myself as a bit of an idiot – it wasn't a glamorous fall. I think that stops me focusing on the things I know are good for me and could help me heal.

Journal Prompt: The dialogue method

A journal dialogue begins with a greeting, then a question and ends with the participants saying goodbye:

A: Who can I have a dialogue with?

B: You can have a dialogue with anyone or anything you want to or need to.

A: But aren't I just making it up?

B: Or are you just listening and recording – why don't you have a go?

A: Well, maybe, thank you.

B: Good luck. I'll see if I can help you.

Journal Prompt: Writing a journal dialogue

Decide who the dialogue partners or participants are.

- Are you going to speak from your whole self (or known present self) or from a part of yourself?
- Do you want to dialogue with someone outside of yourself or a part of yourself?
- Perhaps you don't know who the participants are so you can just call them A and B.
- Perhaps your dialogue partner is not a person at all.

CHAPTER 8

Unsent Letters

Unsent letters are, with dialogues, cornerstones of the therapeutic journal-keeper's repertoire. Whereas dialogues can feel counter-intuitive and require practice and training, unsent letters are more immediately comfortable for most people. This is because letters are a familiar form to most people from the early experience of 'thank you letters' visited on children at birthday and Christmas:

> Dear Aunt Alice
>
> Thank you very much for the luvly hankys you gave me for Christmas. They are just what I wanted. We had turkey for dinner.
>
> I hope you had a nice time.
>
> With love from Susie

When a form has been familiar from an early age, it can subsequently be easily accessed for journal purposes (see Journal Prompt: Writing unsent letters, p.147). However, familiarity with letters is now changing; it is said that the letter is dead, that it is being superseded by e-mails and texting, especially for younger generations. My nieces send me computer-generated 'thank you notes' and I am never sure whether they have painstakingly typed every letter or simply pressed a key to select 'Thank you letter'. But people still understand the 'idea of a letter', even if the thought has a nostalgic cast (see Journal Prompt: Gratitude letter, p.147).

The first unsent letter some children experience is the letter to Father Christmas; it is a letter to express hopes and ideas and wishes. This can be adapted for determining your contemporaneous hopes, ideas and wishes. In times of global uncertainty a 'Letter to the world', expressing your hopes and fears and wishes, can be an interesting letter to write. This kind of unsent letter can be a statement of intention – after writing his unsent letters to the world David joined Amnesty and began writing letters to be sent.

Therapists who would not normally ask clients to write will sometimes suggest that they write an unsent, or no-send, letter. Clients who would look askance at the idea of keeping a journal can relish the idea of writing unsent letters. Writing a letter to someone, even though at the time of writing you know you will never send it, is considered to be a perfectly acceptable thing to do. Perhaps the idea of an imagined reader or recipient, albeit one who will never receive it, makes it a more 'logical', 'normal', familiar, acceptable activity. The idea of keeping a journal can be dismissed as 'self-indulgent' but writing a letter is a normal part of social intercourse and communication.

Personal relationships with letters

Letters were always an important part of my experience and particularly of relationships (see Journal Prompt: Personal letter-writing history, p.147) and this will be reflected in the lives of many clients.

No serious or intimate relationship was ever properly consummated until it was celebrated in epistolary form. As a child I made sure of the continuity of friendships through our family's frequent and lengthy holidays by writing letters. It was not just receiving the longed-for and much looked-for (often requiring daily trips to a distant village post office) replies which was important, it was the writing of them. Although being kept in mind by the recipient as proof of ongoing existence was part of it, it was the sorting and processing of my own experience in the writing that mattered. When I lived abroad, first in a gap year, later as a junior faculty wife, I was sustained by the letters I received from friends and relatives back home. Sometimes relationships developed through letters in ways that they would not have done had we lived in closer proximity.

Letters are a way of continuing conversations over time and across space. This is just as true with unsent letters as with normal posted letters. Through unsent letters the relationship with the self can develop and deepen and new conversations be developed.

Unsent letters in bereavement and grief

In her poem 'The Hooded Hawk', Anne Michaels writes:

> *Colette said, when one we love dies*
> *there's no reason to stop*
> *writing them letters.* (Michaels 2000, p.185)

Unsent letters can be a useful therapeutic device for those experiencing bereavement and grief, and I used them myself following the death of my mother.

Following the event, I wrote my journal entry of arrival as if it were a letter to my mother. Whenever I moved to a new place or a new house my instinct was to write to my parents to tell them about the experience, almost as though I could not really experience it directly until I had filtered it through a letter to someone else. Not having a very visual memory I think there may be some truth in this, or that at least that translating experience into written words made it more vivid for me. The fact that these were sent letters may be less important than that they were written.

The summer after my mother died we went to the US as usual and I wrote in my journal:

> I have always written to her when I have been out of the country – almost my first act on arriving anywhere was to write to her. I would process my first impressions through my letters to her – to arrive somewhere was to tell her – perhaps to tell her that I was separate, away, out of her ambit – but I

was also trying to draw her in, to share, to give her part of my experience.

I also wrote regularly to my father after his shockingly sudden death. It allowed me to continue to have him witness some of the events in my life and for me to recognize how important he had been to me in shaping my thoughts and values. In a way, I wanted him to know how it all turned out and my existence felt more solid as a result of doing this.

> When the older sister of one of my former clients, Amy, was killed in a car crash, Amy took over the care of her 14-year-old niece. Her own grief was complicated by her need to assume the role of mother and help her niece with her journey through grief. As she grieved for her sister and simultaneously became the carer of her niece a feeling of guilt emerged. Survivor guilt is a well-documented phenomenon, but in this case it was compounded by Amy's feeling guilt for taking over the mother role. She felt she was having experiences which rightfully belonged to her sister; somehow she was usurping her sister's role and excluding her.
>
> She wrote a series of unsent letters to her sister documenting the day-to-day experiences of her niece's journey towards adulthood. She also included memories of her own childhood (and therefore of her sister). This enabled her to include and invoke her sister in her experience and process her own feelings through writing. Her niece grew up to be a literate and intelligent young woman and later Amy presented her with all the letters on her 21st birthday. This gesture completed a process for both women.
>
> Amy's letters remained private to the family, but other people have used their writing about loss and grief to reach out to a wider audience.
>
> Four months after the sudden death of her husband in 1975, Jill Truman started writing unsent letters to him. Eventually these became *Letter to my Husband. Notes about Mourning and Recovery* (1988) in which she documents her journey through grief and widowhood and coping with four young children. The book clearly illustrates the tasks of grieving, the adaptations and the steps backwards and forwards through the process. She says in her afterword: 'The Letter was my lifeline. My regular communication with a man whom the rest of the world considered to be dead' (Truman 1988, p.83).
>
> She also knew when it was time to stop writing to him. For seven years the exercise book remained in a cupboard until her best friend was going through a similar process. 'I would like to say to any woman who finds herself suddenly, unbelievably, in the position I was all those

years ago: it will be OK, just keep putting one foot in front of the other'
(Truman 1988, p.84).

There is an increasing number of published memoirs by bereaved spouses
including Joan Didion (2005), Danny Abse (2008) and Sheila Hancock
(2004) which may not ostensibly be written in the form of letters but
unquestionably are an extended form of unsent letters; the writing of
them can be seen to serve the same therapeutic purpose.

Unsent e-mails

Now that e-mail is in the ascendant and hand-written missives are in
decline it may be advisable to consider the possibilities and pitfalls of
unsent e-mails.

It is all too easy to send an e-mail once it is there on the screen –
touching the 'send' button can be an automatic reaction after typing
one's name at the end of the e-mail, which is possibly why 'oops – forgot
the attachment' follow-up e-mails are so frequent. One useful tip is to
write them leaving the address bar blank if it is intended or desirable that
they remain unsent.

Intended recipients

Think about people to whom you need to write (see Journal Prompt:
Recipients, p.148). Recipients of unsent letters can be real or imaginary,
known or unknown, living, dead or as yet unborn; they don't even
have to be people. Some diarists write their diaries as a series of unsent
letters, creating an imaginary reader or companion; this is not a modern
phenomenon.

The writer Fanny Burney (1752–1840) began her journal at the age
of 16 by writing to '*Dear Miss Nobody*…' George Sand (1804–1876)
created a male alter ego in Dr Piffoel to whom she wrote. The best
known example of all is of course Anne Frank who, in 1942, began to
write her diary and said:

> I want this diary to be my friend and I shall call my friend
> Kitty. (Frank 2009, p.15)

The creation of an imaginary friend is someone with whom to share the daily and extraordinary events of life, someone who will witness your life and always be there.

Emotion and unsent letters

Unsent letters are ideal vehicles for discovering what you really feel, for seeing the emotion of the situation without the usual socially acceptable restraints. The emotion has a way of appearing on the page; it's there in the writing and sometimes even more apparent in the reading. Sometimes the first time that clients connect with the emotion on the page is when they read it out loud, when it becomes present in the room, and then is reflected back to them by the therapist. Sadness, forgiveness, compassion can all be recognized for the first time in unsent letters, but the most potent use of the technique can be in recognizing and acknowledging anger.

Anger

Unsent letters are useful for revealing underlying or suppressed anger. We are often trained in childhood to conceal anger; this is particularly true for girls who are licensed to cry and be upset, but not to be cross and to shout (the opposite may be true for boys as a childhood display of anger or a tantrum may elicit the response, 'Oh, he's such a little boy' whilst tears elicit, 'Don't be a cry baby').

Women can be trained to respond in a passive way to situations where anger may be an appropriate response. When written 'to' a person, as in an unsent letter, the anger will tend to reveal itself despite the writer. I have seen this happen many times in clinical work with issues of abuse, abandonment, rejection, in personal and political events. Often the letter writer will be surprised, if not dismayed, to find the anger on the page and to see that it exists. Unsent letters can help people get in touch with their anger rather than internalizing it and turning it against the self (Thompson 2006).

Below are examples of counselling clients who discovered their anger in their unsent letters:

- A wife who wrote letters to her husband who was in prison, was astonished to find her anger on the page when she had no firsthand knowledge of it, had never 'felt' it ('I'm not that sort of person', she said).

- A woman in her early 60s, abandoned by her live-in lover of 10 years, was sunk in despair but able to revel in her anger on the page. She wrote many unsent letters until the anger began to diminish. She eventually got bored with it – unsent letters had done their job.

- A survivor of childhood sexual abuse had to write many letters to her dead father (the abuser) before she was able to tell him she was angry with him ('I don't do cross', she had said for a long time to her therapist). Eventually the need to self-harm diminished as her anger was expressed through the unsent letters.

- A woman who wrote an angry unsent letter to her dead mother suddenly stopped biting her nails after being a lifelong nailbiter. She was able to speak the unspeakable when she read it out loud.

All these people used unsent letters to work therapeutically with aspects of their past experience. In all these examples anger would have been an appropriate response to those situations, but the writers had been unable to acknowledge this at the time (some of them said things like, 'I don't do cross' or 'I'm not an angry kind of person' – but actually the letters told them otherwise). Some were able to become angry from an adult perspective as a result of this process; they became angry about things that had happened to them in childhood. In childhood they had not been capable of understanding that some of the things happening were not acceptable, were not their fault and were not something they had 'deserved' or invited.

These clients were all working in therapy with aspects of their past and the sequellae of unexpressed anger. Unsent letters can also be used in a more immediate sense to work with anger: to express the felt anger of the moment in a non-damaging way and provide much needed catharsis. Below are some more examples.

> Ergul came home from work fuming with anger triggered by a work colleague's attitude. He was still angry when he arrived at the journal group that evening and wrote the following:

Dear Pat

I can't believe you did that. What have you done? Why? Why? What you said and waiting till I was about to leave – no time to do it then. What am I supposed to do? What were you trying to prove? It's ridiculous.

If we have lost that contract because of this. It's not my fault. I'd worked so hard to set this one up. I worked my arse off.

Yours, Ergul

Initially the letter was incoherent, an inchoate expression of raw rage; he was choked by anger but this began to recede as he processed his feelings and was able to see the situation from a more helpful perspective. Reading the piece to the group, he was able to recognize his anger and also let go of it with a rueful:

Well, perhaps he didn't deliberately sabotage my work – there's nothing which can't be remedied with a phone call in the morning.

The group's ability to witness his feelings without judging him or his colleague was a powerful part of his process in being able to move beyond his initial reaction.

Ella, outraged at the service she had received in a restaurant, was full of righteous indignation. She felt slighted, disrespected and ultimately ripped off. Fed up with the combination of apathy and anger which so often prevailed she decided to write to the manager. But she knew herself well enough to know that sending a letter in that state would not be productive or help her make her case. First she wrote an unsent letter in which she allowed herself to express all the sense of outrage at the situation and contempt for modern standards in general. The letter she finally sent was a model of restraint and good manners – modelling exactly the behaviour she wished she had received. The reply she received and the vouchers for cocktails mollified her considerably and validated the process for her.

Not all unsent letters are about the conscious or unconscious expression of anger or the process of grief, though those are particularly significant manifestations and frequently occurring themes. Other themes might include 'love letters', letters of forgiveness (of yourself or others) or the more difficult aspects of self involving shame, guilt or hatred. Other emotions, like fear, joy or anxiety, may also come to light and be worked through in unsent letters. They can be the vehicles for unrequited love or apology or the ideal place to unload guilt and shame (see Journal Prompt: Apology Letter, p.148).

What to do with unsent letters

Reading the letters aloud can be a very therapeutic act, even more so than with other forms of therapeutic journal writing. Letters are a written form of communication with another person; reading them out loud is a way of imagining the communication sent. Having them witnessed by other people, in therapy or in a writing group, is part of this, but reading them aloud to yourself, being your own witness can be equally effective.

However, this is one area of therapeutic journal writing where the destruction of the letters can be an important and therapeutic part of the process. The reasons for doing so could be important.

What is the intention behind the act? Is it to rid yourself of unpleasant thoughts or material (in effect to banish them) or is it to signal a very definite kind of closure? There are various methods of destroying unsent letters:

- *Burning*: In bereavement work, some kinds of unsent letters can be ritually burnt in emulation of funerary rites or even placed in the coffin before cremation or interment. In other processes burning can be important as a way of letting things go, literally, up in smoke and float away on the air. This can be part of a purification or purging ritual.

- *Tear it up, flush it away*: Ridding oneself of unsent letters can have an almost comical aspect as in the woman whose husband had left her who wrote him an unsent letter and then delighted in tearing it up and flushing it down the toilet. The symbolism of the act was deliberate and the laughter as she described it was cleansing. In this way she re-discovered her sense of the ridiculous and recovered a sense of proportion.

Letters to the unborn child

Whilst it is more often pregnant women who write to the unborn child when it begins to kick inside them there is no reason why fathers-to-be should not also find this useful.

Kay wrote regularly to her unborn child: 'Dear Rebecca…' She was surprised when Rebecca turned out to be Robbie, but it didn't diminish the usefulness of having written the letters as a way of preparing herself for the enormous changes in her life. Robbie perhaps received an even more non-sexist upbringing than he might otherwise have done.

Future or past selves

Unsent letters can be a way of expressing compassion for the self, and can be a way of beginning to love yourself again (see Journal Prompt: Letter to a different self, p.148). Sian wrote a letter from her older self:

Dear Sian

You will find that, when you get to my age, these things no longer seem so important. It really doesn't matter now what he said to me then. After all, I know that I was not the problem. You blame yourself so much, you are so hard on yourself. From where I sit I can see all the other experiences and people you have had good times with and who are important.

I think you'll find that you have people who really do matter and who will give you much more love and support. There are people who love you, you know, I do and I know your mother would have agreed with me. You have a tendency to take things very much to heart and to feel the full extent of your pain. But believe me, it will pass.

Be gentle with yourself.

Your loving,

Octogenarian Sian

Journal Prompt: Writing unsent letters

Unsent letters differ from the letters of normal social intercourse by being just that – unsent. The first rule of unsent letters is that you should: **Promise yourself that you will never, ever send this letter.**

Of course you may wish to use this as a first draft for a letter you do send, you may wish to share some of what you write in a mindful and considered way, as always asking yourself:

- Why do I want to share this?

- What response do I expect?

- Who do I really want to know this?

One of the best reasons for not sending unsent letters is that ultimately they are communications with the self.

The second rule of writing unsent letters is that you should: **Allow yourself to be as open and honest as you can.**

In other words, allow yourself to express any thoughts and emotions you feel – even if you would prefer to disown them or do not recognize them or find them unpleasant or difficult to bear.

Journal Prompt: Gratitude letter

Are there people to whom you would like to say thank you? Is there gratitude which you want to express to someone or to something or to yourself?

Write an unsent letter of gratitude – a grown-up thank you letter.

Journal Prompt: Personal letter-writing history

What has your history with letters been?

Have you kept those you receive?

What were the earliest letters you wrote/received?

What is your current experience of letters?

Journal Prompt: Recipients

Keep a page in your journal for future unsent letter recipients. Add to this list whenever a particular person or issue occurs to you.

Begin listing the people who have been important in your life – include those no longer there and those you have never met.

Journal Prompt: Apology letter

Is there someone you would like to apologize to? Or someone you would like to receive an apology from? Write the unsent letter.

Journal Prompt: Letter to a different self

1. Find a photograph of your younger self – write to her – what would you like her to know about what you have learned in your life so far? What advice would you give her? What reassurance does she need?
2. Write a letter to yourself from a wise counsellor – perhaps a future self who can help you to illuminate your current situation.

———•◆•———

CHAPTER 9

Perspectives

Most of the time people can only look at themselves and their lives from a single viewpoint, striving for a linear and consistent narrative. While this can keep us grounded and in touch with our lived reality, it can also prevent us from seeing things in a meaningful way.

We can become very fixed or stuck, unable to see the wood for the trees. Therapeutic journal writing can help to move things to a different viewpoint or even a multiplicity of viewpoints. By exploring life from different perspectives, by changing the point of view, changing the voice, the time, tense or place it is possible to gain fresh insights. Sometimes the shift in viewpoint can help us see things in a new and different way. This can lead to thinking and behaving differently. Changes, subtle and slight or huge and obvious, can all have a significant impact on the way lives are lived and understood.

Perspective entries can change time, person or viewpoint and provide different ways of looking at the same thing.

Time perspectives

Changing the perspective of time usually means projecting forward (to what might be, the exploration of possible futures) or shifting backwards (to what might have been or the exploration of roads not travelled). This type of exercise can lead to people making significant changes in the present by viewing it in the light of the past or from a future vantage point. It allows people to see the possible consequences of the current situation or to illuminate life as it is being lived.

Because it is not possible to live different lives simultaneously, people are faced with decisions requiring them to choose and consequently give up other options or possibilities. People generally do not like giving things up; renouncing or excluding something leaves us feeling deprived and sometimes anxious. Choices which feel hard to make can leave people wracked with uncertainty, feeling under pressure to 'get it right'.

A perspectives entry is one way of thinking about the 'what if…', 'what would it be like if…' and exploring the roads we might take as well as the roads not taken. It can also help to explore the more potent question 'How will I feel if I don't?' Clients who say 'I don't know what to do…' or 'I'm in an impossible position' are ready for perspectives work.

Existential psychotherapist and writer, Irvin Yalom, describes using a version of this technique in talking therapy. In his book on death anxiety, *Staring at the Sun* (2008), he is treating a patient who is beset by regret for past action and faced with a potentially life-changing decision. He says to her:

> 'Let's pretend a year has gone by, and we are meeting again in this office.
>
> …OK?'…
>
> …I begin the role play: It's a year from now… 'Let's look back over the past year. Tell me, what new regrets do you have? Or. In the language of Nietzsche's thought experiment, would you be willing to live this past year again and again for all eternity?' (Yalom 2008, p.103)

This process allowed his client to begin to make some major changes in her life; it confronted her with her own responsibility for how she lived and what was actually within her power to change. In Yalom's words 'The process, however, opened her eyes (and her jail door)' (Yalom 2008, p.104).

This is a way of exploring the question, 'Is my present going to satisfy me for my future as well?' This technique can be introduced to clients by therapists or to students by trainers, teachers or lecturers. It can be used as professional development/self-supervision by practitioners of all kinds. Subsequent reflection can be done by the writer alone or with a therapist, mentor or supervisor (see Journal Prompt: The year ad infinitum, p.159).

Looking forwards

Writing from an imagined date in the future allows you to think about what you need to do in the intervening period and how you are going to live. This can involve identifying changes, hopes and goals (see Journal Prompt: Looking forwards, pp.159–160)

Making decisions

When you have a choice in either your personal or professional life which will somehow affect your future, writing two perspectives entries can help you to think about what the decision might mean. This can help to clarify which of the two paths might be more interesting, which feels right, is more practical, manageable and what the possible but unsuspected disadvantages might be (see Journal Prompt: Making decisions, p.160)

Julia – a decision to make

Julia, a woman in her mid-30s, worked in hospital administration. She attended a therapeutic journal writing workshop when she was facing a binary decision which could change her life completely whatever she did. Her boyfriend had been offered, and accepted, a job in Australia from the following summer and he wanted Julia to go with him. She was very tempted. She liked the prospect of a new and unknown life, the opportunity to live in a different country and culture and to be with Ash. However, she knew that to sell her house, leave her job and say goodbye to her friends and family was a big task, involving inevitable loss, and the lurking thought: what if it didn't work out? Nor was she sure how comfortable it was for her to go as a 'trailing other' when independence and being a woman in her own right had always been important to her. She was also concerned about her mother who was growing older. She felt torn and rather paralysed by the choice, recognizing that it was an either/or decision; it was impossible to live both lives. The more she thought about it the more impossible it seemed to choose one path rather than the other. The decision became bigger and more important.

In the workshop she wrote two perspectives entries, each one projected forward six months to a time after her boyfriend would have started his new job. The first described how it would be if she committed to staying in England, in the same job, same place, same life except with no boyfriend across town. Her mother was so pleased. Most importantly, she wrote about how she felt about not having gone to Australia. Her second piece described what it might be like to have gone to Australia, to be living with Ash and finding a job. She wrote about how strange it was but also how exciting and different. In this one her mother had accepted the decision and even began to plan her holiday in Australia.

When she read them out the contrast was immediately apparent. Her tone, as she read the first one was dull and slightly monotonous, the feeling was regretful whereas the second was joyful, alive and curious. Hearing them read out and accepted by the group was a powerful part of the process (see Chapter 2).

The outcome was…she went home from the workshop and rang some local estate agents to have her house valued.

This is not to say that the writing that helped her to decide or even to work through the decision process, but rather it helped her to get in touch with the feeling level of the decision which she had not previously accessed. In the end this was more about the excitement of the new than the fear of change. Reading it out to the group allowed her to have her feelings acknowledged by herself and witnessed by the group.

Reviewing the future or setting intentions

The date you choose for your perspectives entry might be some time after you know a decision will have been made; it could be the end of the current year (a typical time for taking stock, reviewing and looking back); it could be your next significant birthday or it could be an anniversary.

Some journal writers write an annual review of the year; they find it a way of reflecting on where the previous year has taken them then they are able to make plans and set goals for the year to come.

Projecting forward to the end of the year and writing a review of the year as yet unexpired is simply a variation on this – it's a way of thinking about what needs to happen before the date arrives or making preparations for dealing with expected or inevitable events.

At the end of one year Claire wrote a list of her achievements:

30.12.2006

This year I:

1. gave up smoking
2. taught 16-year-olds who Jane Austen was
3. started my counselling diploma
4. travelled to Spain on my own to visit James
5. wrote (and finished) several short stories
6. did the 3 Peaks Walk.

and then she immediately wrote a perspectives entry for the coming year:

30.12.2007

This year I:

1. learned to drive and passed my driving test
2. passed the first year of my counselling diploma
3. got a permanent job
4. visited James in Spain
5. submitted some short stories.

Her reflections were:

When I read this I notice first that there were several achievements in 2006 after all — I had thought it an undistinguished, drifting kind of year. Then I notice things are still a bit marked out in pass/fail as if everything is a test.

I also notice that everything is very concrete, quantifiable, little emotional content (except James of course, perhaps...), little to do with ME only with externals. I can see that my goals for 2007 are a logical development of 2006.

She saw this as a way of setting her intention for the coming year and by the end of 2007 she could tick several items off the list. Her reflections on the process clarified quite a lot of things for her about how she related to the world:

3. got a permanent job – yes and no. The contracts I have are no longer short term but… I do not feel permanent – Lack of commitment? Needing to see the exit again? I've not yet got the job I want – have not found the satisfaction/fulfillment in a job to feel committed, but then maybe I'm wondering if I want to go to Spain, maybe. I haven't admitted how unsettled I really am.

Preparing for events

If there is a looming forthcoming event or an ordeal to be faced (such as an interview, an assignment, a medical procedure), writing about it from the projected future can help:

- think about ways of approaching it
- reduce anticipatory anxiety
- help to prepare you to withstand a shock
- identify ways of overcoming the problem.

In preparing for the final video presentation on her counselling course, consumed with nerves and stage fright, Claire wrote a perspectives entry in two stages – immediately before the presentation and immediately afterwards.

Before

Oh my god, in a few minutes that door will open and I'll be invited in to show my video to the panel. I've got the tape here, the notes for my commentary. I feel about 11 years old (before grade 3 – performance anxiety, yucky), I wish the ground would swallow me up, there'd be an earthquake so I didn't have to do this and we'd all have something else to think about.

But I know I'm ready – the tape is good, I know it backwards (going through it over and over again really helped – even though I hated even putting it in the machine at first). I could stand on my head and do it!!!! Those people are not my enemies. I can do this.

Feedback: I do feel much better about it having really thought about it, having pictured it. I also recognize it is important for me to really, really, really do the preparation and look at the tape so that it is true I know it backwards – I could be so petrified that I can't even bring myself to look at it on my own. I can now plan times to do this.

After

> The door closes behind me. I'm still here, I've got the tape in my hand and my notes. I did it and I survived. I don't see what can have gone wrong – they asked questions and I was able to answer them – I did speak in sentences and make eye contact. I think I will go to the pub and see if the others are there. IT'S OVER!!!!!!!!!

Feedback: Reading this reminds me that I'll survive – I can do this and then it will be over.

Changing behaviour

Projecting forward can bring people into contact with the possibility of change at times when they are feeling particularly stuck or overwhelmed by feelings.

> Doris, a woman in her 60s, came to counselling at her doctor's suggestion. She had been left by her live-in lover of 10 years and was feeling shocked by her inability to live life as normal.
>
> At the time she was still angry, hurt and depressed by the betrayal and abandonment (he went to live with a woman she knew, they were members of the same Social Club) but she was also starting to be frustrated by the fact that she still felt the same as the day he left; it just didn't seem to be getting any better.
>
> She was getting bored with herself and whilst writing unsent letters had helped her to access her anger they too had become boring. She wrote a perspectives entry projecting forward six months, writing about what she was feeling and what she was doing. When she read it she was so horrified that she might still be feeling as hopeless, helpless and abandoned that she wrote another, more cognitive, perspectives entry.
>
> Here she adopted a new and fiercely active single life beginning with a trip to Greece, a place she had never been before, with an old friend. This was her first holiday since her lover left.
>
> She brought the life she would like to be living into her awareness and made it concrete on the page. After a while she began to take some steps towards making it happen and gave up the habit of grief.

Another way of using perspectives is to help with changing damaging behaviour.

> Paul was suffering from severe chest problems, his doctor had warned him about what his future was likely to be if he didn't stop smoking. At

56 he wasn't ready to give up on life but he was struggling to give up his lifelong cigarette habit. He knew he had to do something.

He wrote a perspectives entry from a year in the future – focusing on what his quality of life would be if he didn't make the necessary changes. It was nothing he didn't know, but writing it down and reading it out loud, first to himself and then to his therapist, ensured that he could no longer remain in denial. This helped him to move from the pre-contemplation stage in the cycle of change (Prochaska *et al.* 1994) to being able to take a potentially life-saving decision and begin the necessary steps to break his addiction.

Sam was struggling with his PhD thesis. He'd done the work, he'd put in the time and his grant had come to an end. It was tempting to walk away at that point and not bother with the final stages and writing up. He wrote from the perspective of having finished the thesis:

January 30th 2008

Well, that's that – I've done it, survived the viva. The questions were fine – what I expected. I am after all an expert on this.

When I think back to last October, when I was ready to jack it all in, walk away, get a job in industry – now I know I did the right thing by staying, seeing it through. Feels good – it's pride too, so everyone can see I've done it.

Feedback: When I read this I know that the right thing to do is to write the damn thesis – that's what'll make me feel good in the end. If I don't do it it's like doing the work and not getting the credit. It doesn't matter whether I stay in the subject after this – but I know I don't want to be another not-quite-PhD – ABD (all but dissertation).

Looking backwards

Life is full of moments when the action taken excludes all other possible actions and so the chosen path excludes all other possible paths. A Steppingstones exercise can quickly address which have been the determining crossroads or decision points which set the course for the next part of the story (see Chapter 5). Exploring the life not lived can help to illuminate the life being lived.

Writing about past events as though we are there again can be useful for understanding things differently – applying adult knowledge to childhood experiences, for example, can heal past slights or hurts. Although we can't change the narrative facts of the past we can shift our understanding of it so that it does not have to continue to cast a long shadow over our present and into the future.

> Elsie got a bicycle for her ninth birthday but it wasn't the bright red, gleaming machine she'd seen in the shop window for months. It was old and black and didn't even have gears. When she talked about it she was still bitter, over 50 years later, the traces of the childhood disappointment still lingered, sedimented in her memory.
>
> She wrote a perspectives entry as if it was her ninth birthday in which there was very little bitterness and the bicycle was not as central as she had remembered. She was able to shift the underlying bitterness when she wrote about the warmth and love she felt on her birthday. She recognized that in a family where there was actually very little money even a second-hand bike represented considerable effort.

Changing voices

Writing in the third person

Changing from first person to third person in journal writing gives a different perspective on our lives. By becoming the omniscient narrator of our own narrative it is possible to develop a new understanding, sometimes making it possible to think about things instead of being overwhelmed by feeling. This can be the next stage following catharsis and incoherence or the way out of them.

Writing from someone else's perspective

Writing in someone else's voice can be both liberating and surprising. It involves writing in the first person as though from the inside of another person's head, writing 'as if I were…' Or being 'in role'. This can help the writer understand different aspects in difficult situations, such as family conflict, and access another perspective. It can find or recover compassion in difficult relationships. Some people may resist trying to see another point of view when they are caught up in disagreement, but through writing in someone else's voice a resolution can be approached.

In a workshop Elaine wrote a piece in her step-mother's voice, about a time in her life when her step-brother had sexually abused her. It helped her to recognize the limitations of her step-mother's mind and her inability to do anything other than defend her son even when he was so patently in the wrong:

> Oh, my poor boy, he must have been hurting so bad. He's not a bad person, he just couldn't help himself. And it was only the once...

Whilst it couldn't change what had happened, Elaine came to a greater acceptance and integration of the experience into her history through this writing.

Writing in someone else's voice doesn't mean that you have to agree with them or condone their actions or opinions but it can help understand why they behave or think as they do. It can help you to understand that you are not responsible for them and what they said or did and it can help to set you free from the tyranny of the past.

> Alison wrote a piece in her brother's voice. He was six years older than her and when their parents died he took over. As the son of the house he had inherited everything and had not even let her have some of her mother's things that were important mementoes to her. She had controlled her feelings of anger and resentment, but was aware that possibly a powerful hatred of him lay underneath. Some years later she wrote a piece in his voice after which she understood the conversations she needed to try to have with him. She understood that this was an ongoing piece of work that would not be quickly resolved.

Looking at your self from outside, from the perspective of another, can be illuminating. It can improve self-esteem and bring the recognition of undeveloped aspects of the self or identify areas for change (see Journal Prompt: Another's perspective, p.160).

Janice wrote from her mother's viewpoint:

> Janice was always looking after things – she'd bring home stray animals which I then had to feed, her bedroom was always a mess but she still managed to find room to do her homework. I taught her to cook so I'd know she could look after herself and now she's a smashing cook. Her daughters know what's right – because she taught them. She can be stubborn but I'd trust her with my life.

This is good for raising low self-esteem even though some people may struggle with feeling that it is 'boasting'. A less intimate version of this exercise is to imagine that a stranger (in some examples it's a burglar, in others it's a private detective) comes into your house when you are not there and looks at what your home environment reveals about you.

> Josef wrote:

>> The person who lives here must be a complete mess – he can't find anything here surely. He doesn't know anything about housework (so I think this is a man on his own – he could do with some female input). There's a nice painting on the wall – an original, abstract, bright colours. But the floor is almost invisible under books, shoes, clothes, papers. The coat hooks are coming off the wall – he's either very busy or a complete div about practical jobs. He reads the Guardian so he's probably a bit left wing. New Scientist mags in their wrappers so he's either very busy or lost interest and can't remember how to cancel his subscription. No photos or anything much personal.

> What struck Josef when he read it was that there appeared to be an issue about time. When he explored it further, however, the issue was not the lack of time but how he used it and he did recognize that he was becoming rather socially isolated. Seeing himself as another might from what they could infer about him from his home helped. He thought about the things he wanted to work on and the changes and priorities which were most important to him at that time.

Perspectives are a powerful way of both opening up our worldview, seeing over the horizons, and of examining things through a magnifying lens.

Journal Prompt: The year ad infinitum

If I had to live this year again and again for all eternity I _____

What do I need to do to make this year as fulfilling as possible?

What do I want to do tomorrow?

Journal Prompt: Looking forwards

1.   Choose a date in the future.
2.   See it in your mind's eye on the calendar.
3.   Think of yourself on that date.
4.   Write the chosen date at the top of your journal page.

Imagine that that day has arrived and you are writing your journal on that day as you normally would.

Write a review of the period between your real present and your imagined future date as if you are looking back over it, note the significant events, relationships, and decisions that have been made. Notice how you feel about them.

What would it feel like to be at that point in the future having lived the intervening period?

Journal Prompt: Making decisions

Choose a date six months after the decision has been made and acted upon.

1.   Write as if you have taken one course.
2.   Write as if you had made a different decision.

Consider how you feel at that point in the future, what your life has been like since you made the choice and what the consequences have been.

Re-read your writing and give yourself some feedback.

Journal Prompt: Another's perspective

1.   How would your mother/sister/best friend describe you?
2.   Write a brief description from the point of view of someone who knows you well.

CHAPTER 10

Opening Up

This is the section where the therapeutic journal opens up. Here therapeutic journal writing becomes larger and deeper, containing everything.

Techniques and exercises become more fluid. This is where the therapeutic and creative purposes of journal writing can become inseparable. The practice from now on represents a relaxation of holding and boundaries.

Whilst some techniques are new we can also apply those described earlier in a more liberated way. We assume in this chapter that the previous emphasis on structure, pacing and containment has become firmly established as part of an inner way of being, that your safety, and that of your clients, students and supervisees, is as secure as possible.

In this section the goals or purposes of keeping a therapeutic journal are more concerned with existential concerns such as 'increasing understanding in order to live as fully as possible' rather than dealing with a specific problem of experience. The kind of writing you are most likely to find in this section is often called 'freewriting'.

Freewriting

Freewriting is also known as:

- Stream of consciousness.

- Writing in flow.

- Free association.

- Flow writing.

- Free-intutive writing.

Freewriting as a time-limited exercise is the way many tutors begin creative writing classes saying it's a way of 'writing ourselves here' or 'connecting with our writing selves' or simply beginning to write. Sometimes there is a prompt or topic but most often it is an injunction and permission 'to write whatever comes'. I recommend that it be the last stage to arrive at in therapeutic journal writing.

Stream of consciousness writing is both a literary and a psychoanalytical term. It was first described as such by the philosopher William James, brother of the writer Henry. This was a family in which the two fields were connected.

> Consciousness, then, does not appear to itself chopped up in bits. Such words as 'chain' or 'train' do not describe it fitly as it presents itself in the first instance. It is nothing jointed; it flows. A 'river' or a 'stream' are the metaphors by which it is most naturally described. *In talking of it hereafter, let us call it the stream of thought, of consciousness, or of subjective life.* (James 2007 p.156)

In literary criticism 'stream of consciousness' is a term used to describe the flow of possibly unrelated thoughts, images, ideas and feelings which flow through the mind of a character, an omniscient narrator or even an author. James Joyce in *Ulysses* (2000) and Virginia Woolf in novels such as *To the Lighthouse* (1994) are regarded as prime exponents of this form.

> (**Author's note:** The first time I typed the words 'stream of consciousness for this manuscript they came out as steam of consciousness – flow, building up, power...)

This type of journal writing is also a state of mind. It is where the deepest work of the therapeutic journal can take place. This is not hierarchical, no type of journal writing is inherently 'better' than another, but freewriting is the place where the writer goes deeper into his or her own psyche. Freewriting can be the most creative area of the journal; it can also be fun.

Free associating to images, ideas, memories or emotion can be revealing, enlightening, or even disturbing. Things surfacing in this kind of writing increase self-knowledge and therefore intimacy which more contained and structured entries may not do.

The psychoanalytical technique of free association, as Freud first practised it in the 1890s, was a technique by which patients spoke everything in their minds, however disconnected, apparently trivial or embarrassing it seemed. The original hypothesis was that following images, fragments and memories which the analyst could interpret would lead to the crucial memory. Furthermore, this would uncover hidden thoughts or memories and lead to understanding and re-integration parts of the self which were previously inaccessible.

In experimenting with journal writing and freewriting in an attempt to gain a deeper understanding of herself, Marion Milner said:

> I would pick whatever stood out in my memory, not just after each day, as I had tried to do once before, but from the whole of my life, from hobbies, from journeys, from books I had read, plays I had seen as well as from moments of everyday living. (Milner 1986, p.xxi)

She is somewhat dismissive of psycho-analysts (although she later trained as one herself) but says:

> I did, however, borrow one guiding principle from psycho-analysis, the principle that when you give your mind the reins and let it rove freely, there is no such thing as irrelevance, so far as the problems of the mind are concerned, whatever thought pops up is in some way important, however far-fetched it may appear. (Milner 1986, p.xxi)

Freewriting can produce an altered state of consciousness, a kind of meditative state, sometimes described as *writing in flow*. According to Susan Perry (1999), the requirements for a flow state are that:

1. Your activity has clear goals and gives you some sort of feed-back.

2. You have the sense that your personal skills are well suited to the challenges of the activity, giving you a sense of potential control.

3. You are intensely focused on what you are doing.

4. You lose awareness of yourself, perhaps feeling part of something larger.

5. Your sense of time is altered, with time seeming to slow, stop or become irrelevant.

6. The experience becomes self-rewarding.

(Perry 1999, p.9)

Writing can induce the state of flow and being in flow has been seen to increase creative output. This makes free writing a useful technique for blocked writers seeking therapy to overcome the block.

Whilst Virginia Woolf's novels are often described as stream of consciousness literature, it is in her diaries that we see how she employed this technique to understand herself and her life: 'Melancholy diminishes as I write. Why then don't I write it down oftener? Well one's vanity forbids. I want to appear a success even to myself' (Woolf 1997, p.116) and:

> Nothing to record; only an intolerable fit of the fidgets to write away. Here I am chained to my rock: forced to do nothing; doomed to let every worry, spite, irritation and obsession scratch and claw and come again... I am writing down the fidgets so no wonder if I write nonsense. (Woolf 1997, p.131)

The reference to the Greek Prometheus, chained to his rock, the eagle removing his liver every day only for it grow again, is striking.

In this kind of writing the central metaphors of your life can appear and be recognized. Recording your dreams in your journal can produce a series of images which warrant further investigation. Some people keep a dream journal as a separate book as if dreams were a different strand of life from everything else. This may be pragmatic because a notebook which stays by the bed is always ready to capture the half-remembered fragments on waking or in the half-light and liminal space between waking and sleeping. Free-associating to the images in dreams can be a way of delving more deeply into our emotional selves and unconscious selves, sometimes allowing the buried and repressed memories or insights to be uncovered.

For many years I would dream about school; in particular an image of the spiral staircase that girls used to go down featured prominently. This would happen at times of movement or transition in my life and it was only by writing about it in my journal, seeing its recurrence, that I came to understand its significance.

There comes a point where we suddenly find that all the things we've been holding separate or resisting begin to surface in the freewriting sections of the journal and it is in re-reading the entries over time that we make sense of the bigger movements and currents of our lives.

> Kay wrote:
>
>> What I say exposes part of me – perhaps I would keep my true feelings, innermost feelings to myself. I am afraid. Yet I must write these things out of me – love, hate, I must disguise, disavow – yet first I must write – commit them on paper as I have never done – get them out then begin to see. When I write the adrenaline flows – like being in love everything seems clearer, brighter more vivid – I cut through the muddy surface, the flattening, repressing, dulling rhythms of everyday life which sap my energy and in my heightened state I see things clearer – from a position which is both below and above the ordinariness of life.

Poetry

Stream of consciousness writing is potentially the most poetic form of journal writing. It is where poems can appear on the page and poetic phrases or images can emerge, sometimes apparently spontaneously. Poetry is after all a distillation of experience and perspective in language. Sometimes images from dreams or dream fragments can represent themselves in poetry – though few writers will dream the whole poem as Coleridge did with Kubla Khan.

Natalie Goldberg describes how she gave two pages of her journal to her class. She had 'pulled out' a poem from them and wondered if anyone else could see the poem. Her students then all included the same line, but they all found different poems. She says 'this is where the depth of the relationship with yourself is so important' (Goldberg 1986, p.157). It's your journal, it's your poem (see Journal Prompt: Found poem, p.173).

> After writing about the frustration of not being able to connect to a 'real' self and of feeling that she was not really fully 'living'. Cathy developed the following poem around the image of a shark's mouth which appeared in one journal entry:

> > The eternal striving, striving
> > For a deeper place,
> > A place of clarity and richness.
> > Rend the surface, tear through layers,
> > Strike at protective camouflage
> >
> > Shark's mouths are ineffective,
> > They hurl themselves at the globe:
> > Mispositioned they make no dent.
> > They cannot learn to swim upside down
> > Nature does them no great service
> >
> > The prize eludes us,
> > captive natures kept from Nature
> > by ourSelves, which from our Selves
> > Conceal the Self.

> 'Somehow,' she said, 'the poem allowed me to cut through the froth and get to somewhere more real and incisive. It's about how I stop myself from feeling and living.'

> Wendy had been writing about feeling lethargic. In her journal the image of fog appeared which became the following poem:

> > I feel the fog within me
> > Damp, clammy, insubstantial
> > It fills me,
> > Swelling my emptiness,
> > Stretching me taut
> >   I could go Pop, Explode, Expire.

Writing in particular poetic forms can impose a structure and fresh perspective on experience. Poet Rob Hamberger wrote a series of poems about the last illness and death of his best friend and he deliberately chose to alternate free verse with sonnets: 'It felt as if I was choosing a form whereby the apparent straitjacket of a limited rhyme scheme would hold me tight, give me a sense of security' (Hamberger 2006, p.132).

Other forms such as pantoums, villanelles or haiku can provide a resolution of form and content. This can be highly illuminating rather than simply restrictive. Sometimes people are 'afraid' of poetry, perhaps because of memories of 'pulling poems apart' from school; a highly structured form will allow them to begin to experiment.

Stories

Stories can also 'grow' in our journals. Burghild Nina Holzer says: 'A short story in a journal is not like a short story. It doesn't necessarily have a beginning, a middle, and an end, and it isn't usually written with intention' (Holzer 1994, p.97).

By trusting the process and writing whatever needs to be written or comes to be written you are allowing stories to grow: 'Many kinds of stories grow in a journal. There are of course the stories of one's actions, and if you look at these actions over several months, they might tell a larger tale' (Holzer 1994, p.100).

Holzer also notices that recurring metaphors, dreams and memories can be indicative of the stories that we need to tell in terms of our own psychological development and growth (see Journal Prompt: Found story, p.173).

Working with time

There are three time frames to shape therapeutic journal writing:

- The Present.
- The Past.
- The Future.

Each of these offers different choices and opportunities to make sense of our lives, increase understanding and develop fresh insight.

The Present

In one sense journal writing is always working with the present. The movement of the pen on the page is always the present, the words we write are in the present. Now. In the moment. The present self writes and becomes the agent for self-discovery, understanding and growth. The continuous present:

- I am sitting.

- I am feeling.

- I am looking at.

However, the continuous present tense is not the most common tense for journal writing. A lot of journal writing occurs in the simple past:

- I went.

- He said.

- I felt.

- It was.

Even if the very recent past is being described – this morning, last night, just now – the tense is past though the action of writing is present. As a language English is confusing – who else is using the continuous present as future (I *am arriving* tonight) as though I'm already there.

WHERE ARE WE NOW?

In order to look further it is useful to discover where we are now by answering questions such as:

- How do we describe our 'now'?

- How do we locate ourselves in the present moment of our lives?

- When did our Present begin?

- Did it begin with an external event such as a move or a change or a transition?

These are the questions that 'The Intensive Journal' (Progoff 1975) invites us to ask when we begin to locate ourselves in the present moment of our lives. The questions begin by eliciting the present moment and extending it to encompass the present period. When you have established when your 'Now' began you can ask more questions (see Journal Prompt: The 'Now' Period, p.174).

The Past

At the opening of book three of *Brideshead Revisited*, the narrator says:

> We possess nothing certainly except the past. (Waugh 1962, p.215)

The past is always with us, it's just not always accessible to us in an immediate way. Practitioners of psychodynamic therapy believe that it is only by understanding, re-possessing and exploring the past that we can become fully ourselves.

They believe that because our past experiences and relationships have shaped us to such an extent change only becomes possible when we can fully understand where we have come from. For other therapeutic modalities it is the here and now which is the stuff of therapy; they believe that therapy is about understanding how we live now so that we can live that now more fully.

Whilst of course we cannot change the 'facts' of the past, we can learn to understand them differently. This can be liberating and ultimately allow us to choose how to live now, in our continuous present. The past can be imprisoning until we really, really look at it again, and through writing and re-constructing our memories we can re-author our own stories. Liberation from the past is part of the therapeutic power of journal writing – by re-storying our experience we enable ourselves to make a coherent narrative of our lives.

Lilian Rubin (1996) makes a distinction between 'actuality', the objective facts of the past, and 'reality', the individual experience of that past. To live fully in the present may mean that some old issues need to be processed.

In her journal poem 'The Child of Yesterday' Janet, a member of a therapeutic journal group, wrote a stanza which recognized this very clearly:

The past that comes to haunt you
in the early hours of morn;
The past that needs resolving
for the new you to be born.

In therapy this kind of technique uses the past as a way of illuminating the present, of understanding who we are now and who we may become. Past selves can be members of the cast which makes up the person we are today; one of the ways of getting to know them is through writing.

ROADS NOT TRAVELLED — ALL THE SELVES I AM

Like Penelope Lively (see p.105) Ali Smith's (2006) protagonist in *The Accidental* reviews her other selves. Her protagonist goes out of her house and sees all the spirits of her other possible selves dancing on the ridge top.

Either of these ideas gives access to a cast of other characters we might have been — and in some sense still are. Whilst thinking about the 'what might have beens' could give rise to a flood of regrets and the sense of lost opportunities, what actually seems to happen is that people recognize the legacy of those days and selves in very positive ways. Sometimes it allows people to let go of regrets for roads not taken, for other people it is an opportunity to re-discover old interests which could be revived in some way to enhance the lives being lived.

> Margaret had long harboured a vague sense of regret that her life was not quite as it might have been and that she was paying for her decision not to marry an earlier boyfriend (who had subsequently become very successful in material terms). She wrote about the life she would have had had she married Mark and all the things she could have and be doing. To her surprise she was not engulfed in feelings of loss and envy of that Margaret-who-married-Mark, rather she found her rather shallow and her life quite dull — the bits that she liked about it were to do with things that she had in her own life anyway. This enabled her to let go of the fantasy of the life-she-might-have-had and more fully live the life-she-had.

> The cast of selves whom Lizzie saw dancing in the moonlight included a younger, carefree, hippy self who danced barefoot through the grass in long flowing Indian skirts. Her description of wild child Lizzie was so

carefree, so full of joy, that she realized that she need to re-gain some of that in her present life and began to look for contemporary experiences and opportunities to bring joy back into her life.

Carry wrote:

> The Carry who stayed in Leeds – long grey hair in a plait, respected lecturer at the Art college…with a pension.
>
> The Carry who never found Ed would have found a man who wanted to marry her young and have 2.5 children in a large terrace house in Leeds. She would have done an MA when the children started school and found a reading group of other articulate competent women.
>
> Carry in Milton Keynes would have tanned sinewy legs from ardent cycling, living in a house which needs minimal cleaning and large windows facing the sunset.

Feedback: When I read this I discover a pattern of starting and not consolidating. I leave bits of myself everywhere I have been like seashells on the beaches of the world.

Journal writing can also help us to make sense of less pleasant images from the past, remove old fears and understand our experience in a different way. Writing about painful experiences in the past can be instrumental in showing any blocks or unresolved issues which are holding you back now; old rules learned in the past could prevent you from doing things in the present.

LEAVING A LEGACY

Writing the stories of the past can be healing and it can also be a way of creating a legacy for our descendants.

> Vera said it began when her grandchild was doing a project at school and came to 'interview' her 'about the olden days'. She realized then that the children knew very little of what had come before and as so many of her friends and relatives had already died she suddenly felt a responsibility to tell the stories of the past. Her daughter, Nell, helped her by getting her to talk about the photographs in the family albums and then helping her to write things down and finally typing them up into a document, 'a proper book' which she could share with her family and which gave her a sense of self.

These family memoirs become therapeutic for the writer and help the members of the family who read them to locate themselves in their lineage, writing these stories can be healing. Sometimes there are family stories which can be brought out of the shadows and understood in different ways or reduced in their inevitability. This sense of continuity is important for us to know who we are and what our inheritance is – once we know what it is we do not have to choose to accept it.

> When Kerry understood that her mother and her maternal grandmother had married men who had abused them she was able to become the first woman in her family for generations to choose a different kind of man.
> She wrote:
>
>> It's taken me a long time to realize why I chose the boys I did as a teenager, why I was attracted to the hard men, they were exciting, the adrenaline rush, the edge of something – of course it was exciting. But now I know it's also that they had a kind of familiarity. That sense of not quite knowing when things would change and it would become dangerous. I used to listen to Gran and Mum talking about Dad and Grandad – 'good men, always in work, always food on the table. And everyone liked them,' but in my body I had to hold the hidden stories I heard – the screams, the bangs, the Friday nights. Tipped into danger, raised voices, raised fists – I never saw it but I heard it and I saw the Saturday morning results. Mum would go to Gran who would say, 'But he's a good man really, like your dad, they can't help themselves.' This wasn't some Victorian prude talking about men's unfortunate (but normal) sexual habits 'they have needs,' this was a mother telling her daughter that her husband wasn't responsible for the injuries he inflicted. I knew something didn't fit, but it took me until Dad's funeral, everyone saying what a good husband he was, to realize it. It's not going to be my story.
>
> Because she knew the family stories she was in a position to make a choice and undo the legacy of the preceding generations of women.

Keeping a journal can be a legacy of a different kind. When the present starts to fade for some people as they get older the record of the past can keep them connected to their lives.

> Joan came to a carers group, it gave her a brief respite from the hard life which was caring for her husband with Alzheimer's disease. In the past they had kept diaries and now she was able to take them out and they could read them together and feel some connection again. It

helped Joan to realize that not everything was lost and their lives had an ongoing thread, the husband she had known and loved was still there.

The Future

In Chapter 9 on Perspectives, we saw different ways of approaching the future and taking steps to live it as well as we can. What are New Year's Resolutions except our vision of our future? Writing them in the journal is a commitment to becoming more the person we want to be – seeing them recur year after year doesn't have to seem like failure but rather a recognition of our aspirations.

In your journal you can create your own future, as you did as a child in response to the question: 'What do you want to be when you grow up?' In some sense the question never ceases to be viable.

Record your fantasies and your daydreams – write the future you want to create. Perspectives are a way of helping to determine your immediate future.

Journal Prompt: Found poem

- Select a journal entry.
- Underline a phrase or image which strikes you.
- Make it the heart of your poem.

Journal Prompt: Found story

- Look back over your journals, scan them for a recurring theme, character, image.
- What is the story you need to tell? How far is it told already in your journals? Can you bring it up to date?

Journal Prompt: The 'Now' period

- When did 'Now' begin? What is this period like?

- Can you see an end to the present 'Now'? Will it come to an end with a planned event?

- What are the significant feelings of 'Now'?

It is a time when _____

PART FOUR

Applications for Practice

CHAPTER 11

What Works for Whom?

Different therapeutic journal techniques are particularly suited to different types of presentation or issue. Some of the techniques described in this book can have particular applications and in this section we look at how practice might be applied. Whilst many of the examples in this section are taken from my own clinical practice, others come from non-clinical settings.

Social worker Clare finds she can use similar techniques in her work training social workers and in her work with clients; primary care counsellor Meena began to run a group for colleagues in which issues began to emerge that she had previously seen with her counselling clients. Writer and creative writing facilitator Jane has begun to discover that the range of people who come to her writing groups have all the human issues to deal with and she increasingly uses therapeutic journal writing techniques as a way in to the authentic creative process.

So, although some people will come for help for the issues mentioned here, others will discover them on the way and the prepared facilitator will be equipped to deal with them as they arise.

Working with physical symptoms

Practitioners who work in health settings find that a large number of their referrals or group members are people with physical symptoms.

Sometimes people run groups with a particular focus. Barbara Statura, a journal facilitator in Tucson, Arizona runs groups for brain injury patients and has discovered how therapeutic they are. However, often there may be a psychosomatic element to the presentation (in all cases it is of course important that the medical symptoms have been assessed by a medical practitioner). A psychosomatic symptom is a physical and real symptom with no underlying physiological cause.

When stress is somatized, for example, the body produces a symptom which is very real and often extremely painful, such as headaches or digestive problems or even unspecific aches and pains. Writing dialogues with the symptom, or perspectives entries for what life would be like without the symptom, are ways to introduce therapeutic journal writing in this type of work.

The most common types of physical symptom presented with a psychosomatic element seem to be:

- Headaches/migraines.

- Digestive problems.

- Backache.

- Throat/voice problems.

- Body pain.

- Adult survivors of childhood sexual abuse often report 'body pain', particularly in genital areas or in the womb.

In cases where people have no voice, either literally (physically/physiologically) or metaphorically (where they feel habitually unheard and disregarded and so cannot speak) writing can help to provide a voice and give respite in the session.

> Suki, a Hong Kong Chinese woman, was referred by her GP after she apparently had lost her voice and could speak only in a painful-sounding strained whisper. After various investigations for physical causes none had been found. Suki was cross about this – she wanted to know what it was that was wrong and to have it cured. She was a highly experienced financial officer but at this time was unemployed. In our sessions talking was hard for her and listening was difficult for me. It seemed that the most important person in her life was her eldest brother with whom she had had no contact since she lost her job in the City.

She wrote him an unsent letter in a session:

> ...I know you want to think of me as a high-flying city woman. I'm not. I live in small flat, I have no job. I apply for jobs every day but when they phone me I can't speak to them. They hear only silence. How can I tell you I am not the golden little sister? I'm so ashamed.

I prompted:

> 'What do you want to ask him for?'

She wrote:

> Please dear brother, can you hear me? Please dear brother will you listen to me? Please dear brother can I come home?

When she read this out her voice rose above a whisper, she cried, but she had begun to find her voice.

Working with chronic illness

Whilst many of the conditions mentioned above may well have a psychosomatic or metaphorical element, others are chronic medical conditions. When patients have been given a new diagnosis, when they have been told about a medical condition which may change the way they live their lives forever, they will inevitably have strong feelings.

These are often a combination of bewilderment, anger, fear, sadness and loss; they need to be worked through. The strong emotions evoked at these times can prevent someone from really understanding what the diagnosis is and what the impact will be on their way of being.

This can have difficult and damaging consequences if, for example, it means that they are unable to engage properly in the treatment and management of their condition. Therapeutic journal writing can help people to manage their feelings and regain some control over their lives. A piece of cathartic writing (p.37–39) can exorcise some of the emotions but other more controlled techniques can have appreciable and longlasting benefits. Often catharsis is the necessary first step to diffuse and see beyond the overwhelming emotional reaction; after catharsis comes reflection, processing and healing.

The feedback loop is a way of introducing reflection and particularly self-reflection from the start (p.35–37).

Dialogues

When people are coming to terms with a new diagnosis or struggling with the management of a condition, writing a dialogue with it can help them arrive at greater acceptance and understanding of what it is and what it means for them. A therapeutic journal dialogue can become a means of overcoming fear, resistance and denial; it is a useful coping mechanism to use at different times

> Jim was a non-compliant diabetic. He attended his appointments but in between he didn't do the things he knew he should to manage his diabetes. He wrote:
>
> **Jim:** Why did you have to come to me now?
>
> **Diabetes:** You and many others you know.
>
> **Jim:** I don't care about them – I want to know why me?
>
> **Diabetes:** Do you really want to know?
>
> **Jim:** Lots of people are overweight; they don't all get diabetes.
>
> **Diabetes:** Some do. Anyway let's talk about you. Why do you hate me?
>
> **Jim:** Why do you think? You know.
>
> **Diabetes:** Try me.
>
> **Jim:** You mess everything up – I can't eat what I want I feel crap people keep telling me to do things and it's your fault.
>
> **Diabetes:** But I need you to look after me, I can't help it. I'm here and I'll only shut up if you look after me.
>
> **Jim:** I see.
>
> He hadn't been able to acknowledge his anger and frustration before which meant he had not been able to take control of his condition and learn to integrate it into his experience.

Anxiety / phobias

Looking at the barriers to functioning that anxiety or a phobia creates can be a way of getting to know it; looking at what the phobia prevents can provide a clue to why it has developed.

Emily, a woman in her early 40s, had developed a phobia about using escalators. As she worked in an office in the City and travelled by public transport this was beginning to cause her some problems and she found her life becoming more limited.

She wrote a list poem:

If I could get on the escalator I would climb to the skies.

If I could get on the escalator I would go down into the earth.

If I could get on the escalator
I'd travel the Circle Line, starting at Bank.

If I could get on the escalator
I'd meet with my friends wherever they plan.

If I could get on the escalator I'd buy myself smart clothes at John Lewis.

If I could get on the escalator I'd take my nephew to the London Eye.

If I could get on the escalator I'd never ever be late for work.

If I could get on the escalator I'd have to take my mother to the hospital.

If I could get on the escalator I'd go up and up and up and not look back or down or fear.

If I could get on the escalator I'd be free and I could be me.

She noticed when she read it, hidden in the list, the line about her mother and began to wonder if that was what all this was about. Although the advantages of being able to use the escalators again seemed to heavily outweigh the disadvantages, there was this one troubling point. She began to explore her relationship with her mother, eventually reaching a point where she no longer needed the phobia.

Depression

A lot of material has been published which advocates writing as an aid to managing or overcoming depression or describe how many of our great writers and thinkers produced great work when suffering from depression. The links between creativity and depression have been long debated and explored and it is worth considering how writing can support a return to health.

Many writers know and understand this and writers including Virginia Woolf (1997), William Styron (2001) and Gwyneth Lewis (2007) have written about it. Novelist Margaret Drabble says:

> I write at least in part to investigate, to ward off, to understand these recurrent dark periods... Many other writers have prophylactic motivations similar to mine, though others strongly deny any connections between writing and self-therapy, just as they tend to deny links between alcoholism and workaholism. (*Guardian Review* 2009)

Some people say that they only keep a journal when they are struggling, in crisis or depressed, others say that their habit of keeping a journal and their ability to write deserts them when depression strikes. Events which represent a rupture of the narrative can take away our normal coping mechanisms.

Lists

When people have difficulty getting out of bed in the morning, when getting out of bed in the morning may constitute the real achievement of the day, writing may well be beyond their capabilities. But a short, structured and contained task may be a starting point for recovery. Such as:

> Each day: Write down three things you have done today. To begin with these may seem insignificant and prosaic:
>
> 1. I got out of bed.
> 2. I went to the loo.
> 3. I went to bed.
>
> Over time their range will expand:
>
> 1. I got out of bed.
> 2. I made coffee.
> 3. I went to the shop.

People stop recording 'I went to the loo' when they have a more active choice.

The record kept over time allows for change to be noticed and a record of healing and recovery to be created; this provides a map should there be subsequent episodes. The task can be enlarged when things start to improve and energy levels rise. Linking feelings to actions is a useful task – becoming aware of and then registering feelings can help to increase the capacity to experience feeling.

1. Got out of bed – felt very sluggish, weary, reluctant.

2. Made coffee – felt good to smell it.

3. Went to the shop – felt I wanted to hide, didn't want to speak to anyone.

Gratitude diaries are another way of re-connecting to life. The repetition of the same things day after day can be part of the process of recovery, but the facilitator can use gentle probing to help to widen the attention when she feels it can help to shift the stuckness.

> Simon moved from a half-hearted engagement with the process when his therapist told him he could no longer put 'coffee' on his list of gratitudes. He was gently provoked to think more about it, to look further at his daily experience, to pay attention to his life instead of simply being caught in a glib repetition; his therapist's interest and support helped him to take more of an interest and ultimately change his behaviour and then feelings.

> Claire felt she was losing a sense of self when she wrote:
>
> | | |
> |---|---|
> | Who am I? | I feel powerless |
> | Who am I? | I feel low |
> | Who am I? | I am me |
> | Who am I? | I feel disappointing |
> | Who am I? | I feel tired |
> | Who am I? | I don't know if I exist |
>
> So we tried a reflective list poem to look at her roles and the different facets of herself:

I am a wife

        I am a close wife

I am a mother

        I am an impatient mother

I am a teacher

        I am an exacting teacher

I am a writer

        I am an unproductive writer

I am a sister

        I am an older sister

I am an aunt

        I am a new aunt

I am a friend

        I am a good friend

I am a cook

        I am a creative cook

Feedback: When I read this I recognize some strengths and some areas to work on.

Captured moments

As coherence returns to a depressed person's sense of self or identity captured moments are a way of registering it in writing and reading. People who are depressed can live in a very grey continuous present where they do not notice mood changes either internally or externally. Writing and reading a captured moment allows people to become aware of things they did not realize they had registered.

Jo wrote:

> Today I went outside for the first time for weeks. I needed milk so I had to. It felt easier than ringing anyone. It had stopped raining but the ground glistened and the pavements were damp with puddles.
>
> I'm turning the corner into Bessie Road, I can hear my feet tap, splash, tap, car wheels shwish. Then I see it, on a doorstep, curled up, like asleep. A black and white kitten, soft fur. I can't resist so I bend down, stroke it, feel it's silkiness, softness against the skin on my fingers, it yawns a pink wide mouth. I hope I haven't disturbed

it, but it feels so small and soft and alive. I feel like I haven't touched anything for a long time.

Feedback: When I read this I remember a kind of joy.

When I read this I notice that I was aware of a world outside myself and it feels like something emerging after a long dark night.

When I read this I notice the word 'hope' – it's not been in my vocabulary for a long time.

The poet David Constantine, during a talk at the Lapidus conference in 2003, refers to 'luminous moments' when talking about his work with disaffected teenagers and it seems to me that this is what captured moments can be – a collection of them can be strung on a thread of the narrative of someone's life, like a string of pearls to glow in the gloom.

Eating disorders

Compulsive eating often includes an element of shame underlying being overweight or obese. Body image is often a problem for women; bombarded by images of 'how they should look', they often fall short of the 'ideal' which leaves them prey to issues of low self-esteem and self-loathing. This results in splitting between the 'good' and the 'bad' selves which implies that clients with eating disorders are ideal candidates for dialogue writing. Dialogue writing can uncover some of the underlying causes and feelings; revealing insights and understanding mysteriously occur when the different voices have their say. This often provides subsequent opportunities for synthesis and integration.

Janice, a woman in her 30s, who had struggled on and off with compulsive eating and weight gain all her life, wrote a dialogue between her 'fat self' and her 'thin self'.

FS: Hello, Thin Self.

TS: Hello, Fat Self.

FS: It's a long time since I saw you, where have you been?

TS: I've been hiding, you know. I'm here all the time but you gave me a disguise so I could still be in the world and not be seen.

FS: What do you mean 'I gave you a disguise'? I gave you nothing, you left me.

TS: You sound as though you hate me.

FS: I do hate you. One day I woke up, looked in the mirror and you'd left me. Everyone wanted you – they don't want fat old me. I'm not the one they want.

TS: But without you I wouldn't have survived. I'm so grateful to you – you keep me safe – you save me from people who want to hurt me.

FS: So you haven't gone away.

TS: No, of course not, I'm still here. After all, I can't leave you.

FS: Why not?

TS: Because I am you, and you are me.

FS: Yes, I suppose so.

TS: I think we need to support each other – if I wasn't so scared I think I could help you more.

FS: If you could be braver, I don't think I'd need to be so fat. I'll try to help you.

TS: Thank you. Let's see how we can work together more.

This provided a way in to her need for 'disguise' and to explore the 'people who want to hurt me' that her 'thin self' had mentioned.

Survivors of childhood sexual abuse

Childhood sexual abuse is more widespread than people would prefer to think – it crosses all classes, cultures, gender. A child's voice is taken away when she is abused. She may have tried to tell someone and been told: 'Don't (you dare) say such things'. Or her abuser may have said: 'If you tell anyone you'll be taken away/no one will love you/no one will believe you/you'll be punished/I won't love you any more'.

Things may have happened to her which she did not then have the vocabulary to name, leaving her mute. And so she was silenced. I know it happens to boys too; I include them in this despite my use of the female pronoun, but in my caseload there have been far more women than men talking about these issues.

The injunction/prohibition can be perceived as so strong that it becomes impossible to speak about it for years afterwards and writing may provide the way back to language and the creating of a narrative. I have worked with many adult survivors of childhood sexual abuse and have observed that the following stages regularly occur in these cases:

1. Writing and not reading.

2. Writing and showing writing.

3. Writing and reading to self.

4. Writing and reading out loud.

5. Speaking.

Eventually conversation becomes possible but the narrative needs to be re-established through writing before this can happen. Writing the narrative through journal entries, breaking it down into small then growing pieces is a healing process of re-integration of self and experience. It may not always be possible, necessary or even desirable to write the narrative of what happened to the child, although often this is ultimately the way that a continuous narrative of the self can be restored.

In the early stages of therapy the following exercises are also useful:

• Writing unsent letters from adult self to child self, and from child self to adult self.

• Writing dialogues with child self.

• Captured moments for happy/unabusive childhood memories ('luminous moments' can exist in the life of an abused child).

Later in the process the following may be used:

• Unsent letters to the abuser.

• Unsent letters to those who did not protect the child.

• Dialogues with the abuser.

• Dialogues with those who did not protect the child.

• Fairy stories.

• Dialogue with the body.

Family/relationship issues

Resolving family conflict, building relationships, keeping channels of communication open are all common issues in counselling and psychotherapy; they are also present when working with people in all other contexts. Shared journals can create a new medium for addressing and resolving these issues; they can also create a record for the future. Robert and Clara Schumann kept a joint diary for the first four years of their marriage in which they recorded and reflected on their daily lives together.

Some couples or families create shared journals at times of transition or conflict and then can continue to use them as ongoing projects to record and relate their thoughts and feelings. They often then report that these have become important tools for strengthening and maintaining family bonds.

In families where conversations about feelings and emotions are not a natural discourse, writing them can be a more congenial, less embarrassing or painful way of communicating. Shared journals are also useful in families where different schedules make face-to-face communication difficult. Shared journals allow everyone a voice. Where someone may feel at a disadvantage because others are more articulate/ fluent in speaking or may have louder voices, the journal offers a space to be heard and to have a voice. In some educational settings shared journals are developed for student and lecturer/tutor to write in. This allows for reflective dialogue throughout the course.

Bereavement

It is perhaps not surprising that poets turn to poetry in the landscape of bereavement. Several poets have published collections about the loss of their spouse, including Douglas Dunn (2001), Perie Longo (2006) and Elaine Feinstein (2007). In these cases the use of poetry is a means of navigating the river of grief and loss; it becomes a way of making sense of the devastating experience they have undergone and it helps them to find a voice again. The poet Danny Abse, however, found that poetry deserted him after his wife Joan's sudden death in a car crash in which he was driving, so he wrote a journal in prose (Abse 2008) which became a radio play in 2009. He said keeping the journal felt like a way of spending time with Joan and was for a time the only type of writing he could do.

Prose writers too have used their craft to understand the human experience of their own grief, such as Joan Didion (2005), Sheila Hancock (2004) and Christopher Rush (2005). Didion's *The Year of Magical Thinking* became a successful stage monologue with Vanessa Redgrave, which gave the author an opportunity to hear her words returned to her in a kind of feedback loop.

The core therapeutic journal techniques can all be useful in working with bereavement and used at various stages of the grief process.

Unsent letters

Whilst writing unsent letters to the deceased is the most common application, one which can be ongoing for years, writing to other people or things can be a highly therapeutic process. Examples include a bereaved spouse writing unsent letters to children or a bereaved child to the remaining parent. In the anger phase of bereavement people write their inchoate, blaming anger to a person, an object or even God.

I have covered the use of unsent letters in relation to bereavement in greater depth on p.139–141.

Captured moments

These can help people to recover memories of better times by seeing beyond the bereavement and the distress of a long decline or the shock of a sudden loss. The loss of a loved one is bad enough but the loss of any recollection of a happy history or an anticipated future intensifies the grief.

Writing from photographs

In the first phase of grief it may be too painful to look at old photographs; the loss is acute and memories only intensify it. Later the feelings change and people can, whilst still grieving intensely, begin to re-possess the happier memories. Writing about photographs is a way of recognizing that the process is usually a dynamic one.

Carol wrote:

> You're laughing, Nick aged about 3 is on your shoulders, his hands in your hair. Your eyes are squinting against the light. I notice your hair, so luxuriant and long (1973, it's how we wore it then). Even last year it was still as dark as it was then – but less of it – styles are shorter now and you were older, we were growing older together. You never lost your colour. That holiday we stayed in the water mill with the millrace still loud at night. You cooked boeuf bourgignon (very sophisticated we were!) and I had to scrub the casserole! (Wonder if they ever noticed the burnt patch which I couldn't shift?!)
>
> We walked and swam and ate and laughed. We laughed, how we laughed.
>
> This photo would have been unbearable before but now I am so very very pleased I have it. I still cry, of course, but we had such good times.
>
> I love you.

Dialogues

These are particularly useful when there remain things unsaid or opportunities for conversation denied or where unfinished business lurks. Dialogues provide a means to resolve some of these.

Addictions

Unsent letters

Writing to the substance or subject of the addiction can seem like a love letter; it can make people aware of just how enmeshed they are in their behaviour. As part of recovery, writing an unsent letter can represent an intention to change, as is the case in the letter to 'marijuana' below:

Danny wrote:

> Dear Mari
>
> You've been my friend for many years, my home has been yours. In the dark times you were there for me and I'm grateful. At first it was a good game we played – Jim, Carol, Me and Jane. Friends together. Then I remember the times when you took me out of myself, when I think I needed you, when Jane split with me. Your

smell, your comforting arms, 'Relax, chill,' you said, 'nothing can ever be too bad that we can't deal with it.'

We flew together, with Susie, when she first came. Now she wants you out too – we need more time for us and she wants, we want to try for a baby.

But it's time for you to go. You need to leave me now. It can't go on. I have to do it alone now. I'll always be grateful and know that I invited you in and now I have to tell you to go.

After next Friday I can't have you in the house again. That's it.

Sorry mate,

Danny

Lists and perspectives

Lists and perspective entries are useful for exploring what life would be like beyond the addiction, how things might change. They can be used to explore what the addiction prevents happening, which can be good things like being able to form relationships or buying things that would make life more comfortable, or bad things like feeling the pain of experience and life. Lists of things that make change difficult can be part of the pre-action stage of movement.

Dialogues

Dialogues can be used to discover what part the substance/behaviour has in someone's life or to explore the relationship with it.

Writing about therapy/treatment

Sessions with a therapist last an hour; generally they occur once a week. Often clients report that they can't remember what happened the previous week. Writing about the sessions afterwards and reflecting later can help. Keeping a therapy journal is one way of remembering and allowing the insights and emotions to be recorded, and thought about later. This can be a deepening of the therapy and offers a way of capturing the experience for review at different times.

Working with bilingual or second language speakers

For people working in a language other than their mother tongue, it might be thought that journal writing in the first language could be helpful. It could perhaps be a way for them to connect fluently with their own experience, even if they cannot communicate it all in its complexity to someone else. If they do not have the nuanced or abstract level of language to describe it to someone else, then it may be that a coherent written account in their own language could help them to isolate the things which are most important in translation.

However, when they have experienced trauma it can seem as though their own language is too rich and overpowering to contain it. Sometimes, as with my Bosnian clients who had been repeatedly raped by Serbian soldiers, it feels too much for them even to name what had happened in their own language. They may also fear that others from their ethnic group would 'understand' and know what had happened to them. The shame is then unbearable. Writing in the second, less nuanced, less powerful language allowed them to put, hesitantly, in almost childlike language, a narrative back together. Perhaps as some people will use a typewriter or computer to write first about traumatic events because it feels more protective than a hand-held pen (see Chapter 1), writing in a second language allows for a degree of distance or shielding which at first is necessary.

Working with low levels of literacy

If someone can write, but not fluently, they can still use some of the shorter types of exercise such as lists or mind maps. The task is to help them find the confidence to write anything at all. This can mean overcoming bad and damaging experiences (often from school days), learning that they don't have to hide their inability to function in the way that they felt others expected. Simon, a sales executive, would dread the meetings where team members would have to read reports aloud to the assembled company; he would work out when his turn was coming and often resort to saying, 'Sorry, mate, I've forgotten my glasses, can you read it?' He had to prepare a case for Occupational Health – including a log of symptoms. We gradually wrote and read back to each other until he felt more confident.

People gain confidence through having their attempts to write valued and not judged. This can lead to development of literacy skills and a more confident being-in-the-world. There seems to be some correlation between a functional illiteracy and anger issues, particularly in men.

> Pete, a middle-aged man, had been badly bullied at school; his educational attainment was very low but he was not stupid. He first came to therapy after he had provoked a nephew to beat him up at a family party. During the weekly sessions he was encouraged to write lists. These were mainly lists of concrete things he wanted to do such as laying a patio, taking his dog to dog training, learning to drive, going to the optician; these were all things that, in his state of almost non-existent self-esteem and depression, had come to seem impossible. Going to the optician, which stayed on the list for several weeks, proved to be particularly significant – the new prescription for his glasses helped him to see the print and begin to check out his actual reading ability, denied and buried for so long. At the end of therapy he said, 'I've read a whole book for the first time in my life, I can help my grandchildren with their reading.' He was also able to tick quite a few other things off his list as achievements.

Working with people who are unable to write

When someone is unable to write (for physical or educational or language reasons) then having a scribe to write their words can be a powerfully affirming act. In the author's own anecdotal experience, I have been aware of this being used successfully in hospices and hospitals; sometimes it has helped people to create a legacy; at other times it has been a way of affirming that someone still exists. The scribe has been able to create a map of healing for people or a map of a life. It has also been used in community group settings where scribes help those who cannot write for themselves. Even though he was unable to read what it said, Isi was thrilled to be given the story of meeting his wife in writing, typed up on a page – they were his words made real. The power of the written word to confer existence is one of the things that makes journals so effective and therapeutic.

CHAPTER 12

Journal Writing in
Professional Supervision

What is supervision?

> In this modern world where pressures to act decisively conflict
> with a fear of being blamed, supervision can provide a much
> needed time to reflect. I personally think that all workers, not
> just those in the helping professions, would benefit from this
> space. (Shohet 2008, p.13)

Supervision is a process 'to maintain adequate standards' of work,
to protect the client and 'to widen the horizons of an experienced
practitioner' (BACP 2008). It is a space for exploration and reflection
within boundaries of time, place and relationship(s).

The supervisor's first responsibility is to the client rather than the
supervisee. All practising therapists in the UK are required by their
professional bodies to have supervision throughout the period of
practice (this is not the case in other countries). Supervision provides
safety and boundaries for therapist and client allows the sharing of good
practice. Other professions can benefit from this kind of formative space
and increasingly it is 'part of the repertoire for most of the helping
professions' (Shohet 2008, p.13).

In this context clinical or practice supervision is a benevolent and supportive relationship and should not be confused with managerial or quality control supervision. Although most of the examples in this chapter are drawn from therapeutic situations they may also be taken as applicable to other settings. Where mention is made, for simplicity's sake, of 'client' or 'clients' this could equally be applied to students or group members. The term 'practitioner' is used to encompass all professional groups.

Supervision, coaching and mentoring are all process relationships and overlap with each other. Coaching is more often seen in the corporate world and mentoring is particularly in favour in education. '... what supervision, coaching and mentoring have in common is a desire to improve practice through some kind of reflection' (Shohet 2008, p.13).

Since writing is both a creative and a therapeutic act, it inevitably means that there are times when difficult, painful or surprising things arise for clients or practitioners. Writers and educators who work in health settings, prisons or even education find themselves working with vulnerable populations; it is therefore not surprising that emotional issues can arise in what might seem the most benign of exercises. Supervision is the place where these occurrences can be explored and journal writing can offer a valuable addition to the other types of supervision. Supervision can take several forms, all of which fulfil the criteria for the professional requirement for therapists and can be used in combination:

- Individual supervision.

- Group supervision.

- Peer supervision.

These can take place face-to-face, on the telephone and, increasingly, via the internet in various ways. Online supervision is a natural development for practitioners whose practice includes writing. In addition to supervision by others, self-supervision is a valuable addition to a repertoire of methods of support and maintenance. Journal writing offers a form of self-supervision and can be integrated into other kinds of supervision. It can also provide the basis or structure for supervision via the internet.

Journal writing as self-supervision

Patrick Morisette, talking about self-supervision, makes a distinction between autobiographies and journals: 'the purpose of the autobiography is to allow counsellors to examine the influence of the intrapersonal and interpersonal dynamics within their families of origin and their current functioning' (Morisette 2001, p.70). Whereas, he suggests, 'journalling is an effective way to identify and track issues that arise' (Morisette 2001, p.74). I would argue that both of these are suitable tasks for the journal in supervision. Ellen Baker says: 'The journal is the ideal place to examine sources of and possible proactive responses to professional distress. The material can then be explored further in supervision' (Baker 2003, p.11).

The relationship with the self is central to self-care; journal writing is a means of developing intimacy with and knowledge of the self. It helps practitioners to stay connected and grounded in their own experience and practice. Journal writing enhances self-awareness, that is, it allows for the benign self-observation and reflection which is essential to maintaining the self-in-relationship.

Keeping a journal of a writing or therapeutic practice is a way of witnessing the work and becomes an integral part of reflective practice. It differs from any formal record-keeping in that it is not focused on content or process but rather is a free space in which to notice connections, delve deeper into the relationships, reflect on and explore the group process. In this way a practitioner narrative develops and can be referred to in the future. Keeping a supervision journal separate from any case notes or process notes has been advocated by various people as a response to the increasingly litigious society in which we practice. However, in the UK and USA personal journals can be subpoenaed as evidence in legal cases.

The therapeutic journal techniques described elsewhere in this book can be used in self-supervision and provide opportunities to see things differently and to help clarify thought.

Writing a journal of your practice is a way of witnessing your work with clients; it can become an integrated part of your reflective practice. It differs from client notes in that it is not focused on content or process but rather is a free space in which to notice connections, delve deeper into the relationship and look at what is going on for you. It is a place where the practitioner can develop a narrative. A supervision journal is

where work with different clients can be brought into focus together –
and where they can be separated from each other.

Preparation for supervision

One way of making the most of a supervision session is to write about
it beforehand. Both supervisor and supervisee can track their own
feelings and developments about the supervisory relationship through
a supervision journal as well as processing the work they want to talk
about.

Individual supervision

Cathy wrote about her relatively new relationship with her supervisor:

> I do not want to go to supervision: I do not know if it's useful. I do
> not know what the relationship is like between us. I find her slightly
> condescending, I feel we do not understand each other. After last
> time I felt angry and rather upset by the session – I feel a bit resentful
> for paying money for that hour.
>
> What to say in supervision? I had a little insight last week: in the
> last session she said something about my client seeming vulnerable:
> that I was somehow protecting her. I denied this at the time and
> suddenly realized last week: it was I who felt vulnerable, in need of
> protection in terms of my relationship with my supervisor.
>
> I felt bullied by her: but I presented this in terms of feeling she
> was encouraging me to bully my client. The client acts as a shield for
> what is going on between us. We seem to reach an impasse of lack
> of understanding where linguistic and semantic fields are no help.

After the session she wrote:

> In the end nothing was as bad as I feared: she was much nicer to me,
> almost warm, encouraging but challenging me to take the thoughts
> further. We generated dialogue and I was able to talk about my
> client again. But we didn't explicitly talk about last time. I'm not sure
> how, or if I need to – I think I can feel something developing which
> I know to be good for me, challenging but I do not have to be so
> afraid. I need to ask her what she means by 'co-construct'? is she
> talking about collusion? What am I colluding with?

Jenny would come to supervision with pages of case notes which she used to tell the stories of her clients. The time would go by trying to create a narrative of her clients' lives which somehow seemed to leave her on the outside. We developed a range of questions for her to ask of herself before she presented a client and she found that writing the answers gave her a more coherent approach. They included:

- What do I want from presenting this client?

- What are the significant points in our relationship?

- What is she for me?

These helped her to mature as a practitioner and reflect more effectively on her own work rather than being carried away by client stories.

Group supervision

Many supervision groups open with a bid for time. A pre-session journal entry can help to prepare you and indicate what are the cases/issues you might want to bring to the group and what you are looking for as a response from the group. As so often a little journal work can help us to clarify what we know and what we don't know – in other words, the supervision journal can help us to identify the questions we need to ask.

June wrote:

> Supervision group this afternoon. I wonder if I should ask for some time for P:
> I'm finding it difficult to like her but I'm not sure how the group can help – it feels too unimportant. I wonder if the group would think so too. I wonder if I'm afraid of exposing my 'not liking' a client. Aren't we supposed to like them?
> We only have one more session – if I don't take it to supervision I think I'm just wanting the contract to end, to disappear, to forget her.
> I do need to take this – I do want to bid for some time – I think P needs me to do it.

Feedback: It was only when I wrote that that I understood that I needed to take this to supervision – it brought to consciousness some of my resistance. If I hadn't written I would have let myself off and let P fade away, thankful not to have to think about her.

Peer supervision

Where the members of a peer supervision group or in pairs are also open to journal writing it can be adopted as part of the session with an agreement to share and take turns. This is similar to the idea of writing buddies (Goldberg 1986) where both parties can support and encourage each other in their writing and in their work.

Identifying/working with countertransference

Countertransference is when thoughts and feelings from previous relationships or situations in the practitioner's life become revived in the present therapeutic relationship. Learning to work with this is useful in different settings for many practitioners. Using a journal to explore these themes and occurrences can be a powerful way of working through this material so that it does not intrude into the work or overcomplicate relationships in a group.

> Lily, a 36-year-old therapist working in primary care, had been aware of strong feelings in a session with her client, a 60-year-old depressed woman. Lily wrote in her journal:
>
>> I was suddenly aware that I was feeling quite helpless and even a little scared. J was talking about her daughter and how her lifestyle was not one she could approve of; I found she was quite disapproving. We'd been building up quite a good alliance, had identified goals, discussed the contract which I'd explained quite clearly. I sensed her to be a bit resistant, and thought that maybe this wasn't going to be a big transformation for her but it had seemed worth contracting. She was older than me, had worked in the health service all her adult life so there were expectations. I recognized this as my stuff but not paid it much attention – it's happened before and things turn out OK. But the sudden sense of helplessness and some fear...
>> Where does that come from?
>> And suddenly I know – it's that old mother–daughter stuff which I'd dealt with in my own therapy in great detail. I was suddenly again the daughter who wanted her mother's approval...up it comes again. Oh mother, I can see a bit in J the cost of withholding your approval.
>> And I know that J is not my mother and my feelings about my mother belong elsewhere – in my journal, in my therapy and not in J's therapy sessions.

Her journal allowed Lily to process the countertransference and so proceed with J's therapy knowing that she had work of her own to do. In some cases it can tell us that perhaps we need to go back into therapy or take a particular issue to therapy. Self-supervision and journal writing is not psychotherapy even though it undoubtedly is therapeutic – it is, however, helpful in showing us where we need to pay attention and perhaps do more work on our own issues. Some models of supervision will allow a greater space for personal issues of the practitioner than others which will only deal with their own issues insofar as they impact on the client work.

Journal writing as a way of keeping client stories (and clients) separate

A supervision journal can help us to work through times when two clients evoke similar feelings in us, or when they become enmeshed in our minds and hard to separate between sessions. Writing short character sketches about each can help to fix their separate identities, as can writing physical descriptions or pen portraits. As someone with a poor visual memory but a good memory for words, I find it helpful to write a short description or mnemonic to identify clients. This is true in both group or individual settings. Sometimes acrostics are the perfect aide memoire.

Dark-haired

Angular

V-shaped brows bent

Inclined to loud ties

David

Captured moments

Captured moments (Chapter 6) allow you to notice and reflect on particular times, interactions, relationships or stories which may otherwise escape our notice or conscious memory. They also offer an opportunity to re-visit particular times and reflect on our own practice (see Journal Prompt: Captured moments, p.123).

In a world where the expectation is that therapists will see five or even six clients a day, and other professionals even more, it becomes increasingly difficult to give complete attention and remain fully present with each one. Something can get lost in the process and journal writing can help with the attempt to recover it and to keep the different stories separate.

Cathy wrote:

> You are my last client on Tuesday. The room is filled with the imprint of previous sessions and I am ready to go home. Usually you come and we talk and you go and it's not clear that anything much happens. But now something does.
>
> I watch you and listen to you as you pour out your sadness. We are enveloped in it. You are dressed in your normal smart pleated skirt and twinset but your face has lost its well-pressed, immaculately made-up appearance. It's a bit shocking, I'm seeing you naked. I'm momentarily distracted by thinking about where you can go to repair and recover your façade before returning to your world. I think I wanted to go, to escape – which of course I can – the sadness was so raw and so unexpected – for a moment it was unbearable. Your eyes hold me as if you want to be sure I stay there. I realize we have moved to another level of our work and relationship and your relationship with your pain.

Unsent letters

Learning from our clients, students or supervisees can be consolidated in a supervision journal. As a clinical supervisor, writing unsent letters (Chapter 8) to a supervisee can help me understand what I wish to communicate. It can also help to understand where the supervisee is. As a supervisee I have used unsent letters to process supervision sessions, particularly when there were difficult moments which I couldn't process in the session.

Unsent letters to clients enable us to look at the relationship and the issues and reflect from outside the room. Writing unsent letters can be done after the contract with a client has finished or whilst it is ongoing. I wrote the following unsent letter after a few sessions with a client with whom I was feeling increasingly stuck and I was aware of a level of frustration whose source I couldn't identify.

Dear Anna

I've been thinking about our session this afternoon. You seemed down again today. This felt different from the last time me met (which I know was a while ago – you cancelled our last meeting – you left a phone message for me earlier that day.) I suppose a lot of time had elapsed – plenty of time for things to change or not to stay the same.

You were very angry again – angry with brother, angry with sister and especially angry with mum. I felt a sinking feeling as the anger filled the room. Does your anger cover your own despair? There was no room for me.

I felt drained by the end of our session. Drained and a bit hopeless. Is that how you felt? How do you feel after our sessions – is this it – is this why you cancel some? Does it feel unsustainable?

I wonder if I can say some of this to you – perhaps that would help.

I remember your energy of the previous session – that was what felt different.

I hope to see you next week.

All good wishes, Kate

Writing this helped me to realize that I was feeling rejected (that 'poor me' sense) – *there was no room for me* – said a lot. Later I was aware of a similar feeling with a client in another practice and in my supervision journal I was able to explore the similarities and differences within the two cases. In the second case I was able to identify my own process of being tempted into a stern but caring mother role. Reflecting in my journal I could see that my frustration was about how he was 'wasting his life'. I also noticed that I felt both clients were rejecting what I had to offer as a therapist. I could then take this to supervision and with my supervisor look for different ways forward.

After a contract with a client has ended unsent letters can be a way of reviewing the work and processing any ambivalence or unfinished business with it. Where we may have lingering uncertainties about how we managed a case, unsent letters allow us to look again and think things through in a different way (see Journal Prompt: Writing unsent letters, p.147)

The following are examples of how counsellors used unsent letters as self-supervision to increase their understanding of the relationships with their clients past and present and to develop their understanding of their practice:

> In Wendy's first therapeutic writing group there was a woman whom she experienced as particularly demanding and judgemental. She wrote her an unsent letter in which she was able to express her feelings and then to come to see the student in a more compassionate way. She recognized that she was projecting some of her insecurities of being a beginner facilitator and allowing herself to feel criticized and defensive.

> Andrew wrote an unsent letter to a client with whom he had ended the work and subsequently experienced what he thought might be unseemly relief. Despite having talked about it in supervision he was left with some doubts. The letter allowed him to see that the client had not been able to accept what he had to offer and was suffering from chronic loneliness which was not treatable with counselling.
>
> Andrew wrote:
>
> Dear V
>
> I'm sorry but I cannot remember your name. I can see you, remember the warmth of the room and the noise of your television sets.
>
> I had been warned that it might not understand everything you said. In fact I could only understand about 1 in 4 words. The thing is it was such hard work listening to you, not tiring but boring. By the third session you refused to turn off the television in your living room, you had another on loudly a different station in a nearby room. I was irritated that you would stop focusing on the session and make a telephone call. I got that you were lonely.
>
> By the fourth session I learned that I was as sure as I could be that your main issue was loneliness not bereavement.
>
> You were too much like my father, not in looks, but in a kind of self-contained and unneeding way.
>
> Yet when I left you followed me out and waved me goodbye.
>
> I was so relieved when our sessions ended, and guilty for feeling so relieved that it was over. The time we spent together I hope was helpful to you. My feelings though are irritation and relief; irritation

at your lack of interest and involvement in the sessions, and yes I feel used and manipulated, and relief that it is over.

I want to say to you that I can listen and I can hold silence. Why then do I feel guilty at my very quick agreement with my in-house supervisor that the sessions should end.

Yes I did have a final session and I still remember the pleading look when you realized that I would not be returning.

I wish you well and I hope you have found companions, it's just I wasn't one of them.

Best wishes, A

Another counsellor Stephen, felt that he usually managed to let clients go at the end of their contract. However, he tried this and found it helped him to re-integrate the experience and learning of one particular client, someone who had touched him deeply and whom he had unconsciously continued to hold.

Annette wrote:

Dear Pam

It's many years since I saw you last, but on occasions, I find that you come into my mind. When this happens a smile comes to my face or I feel it open up within me. I remember how angry you were, and rightly so, with other people and with me. This was new to me in the counselling room, to feel the blade of anger pass over my skin. I remember you said to me that you held the belief that you could only trust family…and yet you trusted me…a beginner counsellor. It was tough for you, so much pain, so much loss and it was tough for me too. I was afraid that you would take a step too far, take your life. I was afraid of the consequences for me and those close to you.

I didn't want you to die. I was and am fond of you.

You taught me so much and you gave it to me straight, 'You're telling me I shouldn't depend on you, but I needed to depend on you! You're telling me I was wrong to do that!' I feel very emotional as I write this. We journeyed together and as separate people. I know that you wanted to stay in touch with me after I left and I have often come back to that question that I never really addressed. I avoided it, perhaps because I felt that I needed to give you an answer in the moment, rather than giving myself time.

We had many things in common but our lives were so very different. You enriched my life and I know that I made a difference to you at that point in your life.

I hold the memory of you with me.

Thank you, courageous Pam.

Love A

Dialogues

As I outlined in Chapter 7, dialogues can help us to think our way forward, to access different points of view and to hear our own thoughts more clearly. In professions such as therapy in which relationships with clients are central, there are inevitable times when the work feels stuck, the practitioner may want to move things on but doesn't know how or why the work feels at an impasse (perhaps the practitioner him or herself has reached an impasse). At times like these writing a dialogue with stuckness can shift it. It can help find the energy in the work again and to re-direct our attention. When work with a particular client hits a wall and sessions feel stale and unprofitable a dialogue is one way to look more closely at what is going on:

Cathy wrote:

C: Hello Stuckness. You were very present with M today – you've been in this piece of work for a while I've noticed.

S: Why are you so impatient? – when you stop listening properly you leave me no choice, you practically invite me in. I saw you looking out of the window at that magpie on the fence.

C: That was you distracting me.

S: How do you think M was feeling?

C: She was talking as usual, I've heard it all before, the husband, the daughter in Australia, the hip pains.

S: Yes but she doesn't know you've heard it before,

C: I'm sure I've told her.

S: you didn't today – are you turning into a nodding dog?

C: No, I'm not, well, I don't mean to be. So are you saying I wasn't giving her my attention?

S: I sure am. I think you need to come back into the room, not go flying with the magpies that were outside the window (not superstitious are you?) and ask yourself 'Why is M here? What does she want from me?' You might even need to ask her to tell you. Just because she reminds you of your great aunt Hilda doesn't mean she doesn't want to talk to you.

C: Thank you – I think I needed reminding of a few things. Let's talk again. Goodbye.

S: Goodbye

Dialogue with client

This is an obvious exercise but perhaps more useful as a review of the work done than as a dialogue with current clients. Although it can help the practitioner to clarify her own viewpoint, there is a danger that putting words into a client's mouth can fossilize the work in subsequent sessions. Obvious though it may seem, when dialoguing with current clients, the writer should remember:

- Every voice in the dialogue is her own.

- The words written in the dialogue did not actually come from the client.

Dialogue with internal supervisor

The internal supervisor is what, within her own mind, guides the practitioner's reflection on her work. Psychotherapist Patrick Casement says:

> The internal supervisor has origins that derive from before the experience of supervision and its development continues far beyond it. (Casement 1994)

A dialogue with an internal supervisor offers a way of strengthening that inner reflection which maintains a healthy relationship with the work. Such dialogues will often begin with a question such as:

- What am I missing here?

- What am I really hearing her say?

- I wonder what can be underlying this presentation?

- What in me is stopping me from listening properly?

The internal supervisor now represents all the practitioner's previous experience, reading and training and can serve to remind her what she already knows but has allowed herself to forget or access at this time.

Dialogue with practitioner self

Some people find that their 'professional self' or 'practitioner self' has a different agenda from their private self. Writing a dialogue between the two parts is a way of understanding this.

This can be helpful in making decisions and working through career changes or transitions as well as organizational issues. It is also something to be used from time to time to look at the life/work balance:

Cathy wrote:

C: Are you satisfied by your work at the moment?

PS: What do you think? I wonder why you are asking me this.

C: That's typical of you, isn't it? I ask you a question and you answer with a question – you deflect it away from yourself every time.

PS: It's my job. And you aren't being very helpful when you ask those questions – it's just distracting and I've got too much to do to be distracted right at this moment. The contract comes up for renewal, I have to make a presentation, get the figures, finish the discharge letters, complete the core forms. And you ask me if I'm satisfied. Instead of having this conversation I should just get on with those things.

C: So when are we next going to have time to play together?

PS: PLAY? Are you crazy. I can't play, I don't have time to play. With all this to do play is the last thing on my mind.

C: You are telling me to go away and leave me alone.

Feedback: When I read this I recognize how overwhelmed and rather swamped I am at the moment. I need to really look at what I've got to do and work out a more manageable way of doing it – I also need to work out when I can play.

When I read this I'm interested in the last sentence and know I need to look at what that means.

Supervision is an essential part of reflective practice for practitioners and a valuable form of support for what can often be an isolated role. Journal writing as self-supervision is a way of making supervision available and accessible when there is no one to listen; it provides an immediate way of processing difficult or perplexing experience.

Journal Prompt: Self-supervision – Captured moments

At the end of a day or week of client work let yourself think back over the period, notice what comes to mind. Who stands out in your memory? Are there particular moments which stand out? When one of them finally rises to the surface hold it there and begin to write a captured moment:

Write in the present tense, invoke the senses. Notice what your feelings are.

Journal Prompt: Self-supervision – Unsent letter

Think of a client whom you still remember, think about how you ended, what you did together, what the work was like. Think about your feelings towards the client as they were then and what your feelings are now. Remember what it was like being in the room with them.

When your chosen client has come into focus, begin to write an unsent letter to them.

Think about what you would like to say to them about your work together, what you remember, how you felt.

- Do they remind you of anyone else in your life?
- What did you learn from your work together?
- Is there anything else you wish to say to them?
- How do you want to say goodbye?

Afterword

Dear Reader

It's time to say goodbye and wish you well with your therapeutic journal writing practices. Thank you for accompanying me on this journey through this book. My hope is that you will have found ideas, techniques and applications that you can now use with confidence and conviction in your different areas of work. I hope your clients, students, supervisees and colleagues will be beneficiaries of your experience and that you will use therapeutic journal writing as a professional resource for yourselves.

Just remember I'd love to hear from you and other readers about how you have used and developed this work, how it works for you.

Enjoy the wisdom of the journal and remember to Trust the Process and the Pen.

Kate L. Thompson

List of Journal Prompts

Chapter 5 Steppingstones

Chapter 6 Description and Deeper

Chapter 7 Journal Dialogues

Chapter 8 Unsent Letters

Chapter 9 Perspectives

Chapter 10 Opening up

Chapter 12 Journal Writing in Professional Supervision

About the Author: A Personal Journey from Diary to Therapeutic Journal Writing

My first diary was a Letts schoolgirl diary for 1969; I was seven years old. It was pocket-sized with red plastic covers and onionskin paper pages, and all the kings and queens of England on the endpapers. I still have it and I can see a familiar self:

Thursday 23 January 1969: Mummy said I was a trial.

Monday 12 May 1969: Started to type a story.

Thursday 4 December 1969: A perfectly ordanary (sic) day as Thursdays go rather a good 1.

Later I was given a Boots Scribble Diary, a week to view A4 format. Later still (1978) I graduated to page-a-day diaries with narrow lines. Some of these volumes have entries all the way through, others peter out in February or later; the blank pages still stare reproachfully at me. Diaries or date books soon became too prescriptive for me – the guilt-inducing relentlessness of the pages' march through the year. Even as a child I knew it was not reasonable to allocate the same amount of space to each day of the year; after all, a day on which 'overslept, took umbrella' was worth recording is not the same as a day on which 'went up Crinkle Crags and on to Bowfell. It was great' is the entry. Some days would not merit four inches or whatever the daily allowance was, and the remaining white space starkly indicated the paucity of my existence, or lack of time before bed. Other days could not be compressed into the given space, but would spill over date lines with their uncontainable joy or despair or passion of one kind or another. In those days, if I got behind it never seemed possible to 'catch up'; as a child life is lived in the continuous present and experience evaporates very quickly from memory (especially the undramatic kind which much of life and therefore the material for our journals consists).

In those days such books were called diaries and the activity was 'keeping a diary'; when I escaped their confines I called my new books journals and became a journal keeper (a defining noun – it is only recently that I have become accustomed to the active verb 'to journal'). My journals were filled with description, catharsis and narrative. They were not written every day, but sometimes they were, and the day filled the amount of space on the page it needed. Looking back I can see that there was always a therapeutic element to them – learning to name feelings on the page helped me to bear the more difficult ones; recording experience gave me a sense of myself and my life. This begins to emulate the transaction of therapy where a client finds herself known and accepted by the therapist and sees herself reflected back.

The first book I came across suggesting that there were different ways to write in my journal was, ironically, *The New Diary* (Rainer 1977). I was living in Boulder, Colorado: a new city, new country, new continent. I was pregnant, still grieving my father's death and wanting to make sense of my own world. I was immersed in language through my voracious reading, my English Language lecturing and my sporadic bursts of writing. At the same time as I discovered *The New Diary* I also discovered *Writing Down the Bones* (Goldberg 1986). Synthesizing bits of those two books into a method seemed to bring me back into contact with my self and help me restore the fractured narrative of my life.

Sometime later, when my life and my sense of self were again in turmoil and in danger of fragmentation, I articulated that writing it all down helped me to make sense of it, holding the order of things straight when they appeared a great big jumble threatening to overwhelm a fragile sense of self. As soon as I said it I recognized the powerful truth of it. Writing things down helped me to give things a structure and order, to restore a chronology and sense of perspective, and locate me in my self. These things can be lost when we are in turmoil, or more severely, trauma. This was when I openly acknowledged the therapeutic and healing potential of journal writing, and understood that it worked for me.

A few years later I was in Boulder again and I discovered the Center for Journal Therapy and Kathleen Adams in Denver. By then I'd trained as a counsellor and it made sense to combine counselling and journal writing. At that time no one had suggested to me that such a thing were possible.

I'm a stationery junkie. I once bought the entire stock of a particular leather-bound notebook from David's in Cambridge because I couldn't bear not to; I lusted after them, I wanted to possess them – they were the answer (I saw a shelf of uniform notebooks filled with stories of my life and holding the wisdom I would gain if I had them. I think I saw them as being able to offer me a kind of order and coherence I aspire to). They were beautiful, they smelt good and felt good too, I imagined how they would transform my writing. I believed I would commit to my writing (and myself) in them, they would make me a real (journal) writer. I've written in several, several remain in the cupboard, I even gave one away as a present. However, the truth was I got bored with using the same notebook and I realized, at last, that the notebook does not make the writing and part of the adventure is choosing a new and different notebook each time.

This book is an attempt to convey to other people some of what I have learned about the practice of therapeutic writing from my own personal and professional journey. In the course of this journey I have been able to reflect on the place my own journal writing experience has in my life and how I have applied my personal learning and the theory that has developed to my clients, students and supervisees, both individually and in groups. At the end of one group a counsellor said to me: 'I definitely believe in therapeutic journal writing now.' It is in some ways a matter of faith and 'doing is believing' – but slowly the evidence begins to stack up to show that we are right to have faith in the power of writing and the therapeutic benefits of journal writing.

References

Abse, D. (2008) *The Presence*. London: Vintage.

Adams, K. (1990) *Journal to the Self: Twenty-two Paths to Personal Growth*. New York: Warner Books.

Adams, K. (1993, 1998) *The Way of the Journal: A Journal Therapy Workbook for Healing*. Baltimore: Sidran Press.

Adams, K. (1999) 'Writing as therapy.' In *Counselling and Human Development*. Denver: Love Publishing.

Adams, K. (2006) 'AlphaPoems.' In G. Bolton, V. Field and K. Thompson (eds) *Writing Works*. London: Jessica Kingsley Publishers.

BACP Information sheet S2 (2008) *What is Supervision?* Available at www.bacp.co.uk, accessed on 23 May 2010.

Baker, E.K. (2003) *Caring for Ourselves: A Therapist's Guide to Personal and Professional Wellbeing*. Washington: American Psychological Association.

Baldwin, C. (1977) *One to One*. New York: M. Evans and Company.

Bird, I. (1996) *A Lady's Life in the Rocky Mountains*. London: Virago.

Bolton, G. (2010) *Reflective Practice*. Third Edition, London: Sage Publications.

Buzan, T. (2006) *Mind Mapping: Kickstart Your Creativity and Transform Your Life*. London: BBC Active.

Cameron, J. (1997) *The Artist's Way Morning Pages Journal*. Los Angeles: Jeremy P. Tarcher.

Casement, P. (1994) *On Learning from the Patient*. London: Routledge.

Center for Journal Therapy, The (2007) *The Power of Writing*. Available at www.journaltherapy.com/power_of_writing.htm, accessed on 23 October 2009.

Clarkson, P. (2004) *Gestalt Counselling in Action*. London: Sage.

Didion, J. (2005) *The Year of Magical Thinking*. New York: Knopf.

Dunn, D. (2001) *Elegies*. London: Faber and Faber.

Etherington, K. (2003) *Trauma, The Body and Transformation*. London: Jessica Kingsley Publishers.

Evans, C. (2006) *Burning the Candle*. Ceridigon: Gomer Press.

Feinstein, E. (2007) *Talking to the Dead*. Manchester: Carcanet Press.

Fennell, M. (2001) *Overcoming Low Self-Esteem*. London: Robinson.

Field, V. (2006) 'Running groups.' In G. Bolton, V. Field and K. Thompson (eds) *Writing Works*. London: Jessica Kingsley Publishers.

Frank, A. (2009) *The Diary of a Young Girl*. London: Puffin.

Gilbert, P. (2005) *Compassion: Conceptualisation, Research and Use in Psychotherapy*. London: Routledge.

Goldberg, N. (1986) *Writing Down the Bones*. Boston: Shambala Publications.

Guardian, The (2009) 'Chance is a Fine Thing' 20 March, p.20.

Guardian Weekend (2009) 'Experience' 7 February, p.12.

Guardian Review (2009) 'The Missing Piece' 4 April, p.20.

Hamberger, R. (2006) 'Why sonnets?' In G. Bolton, V. Field and K. Thompson (eds) *Writing Works*. London: Jessica Kingsley Publishers.

Hancock, S. (2004) *The Two of Us*. London: Bloomsbury.

Haynes, J. (2007) *Who is it That Can Tell Me Who I Am? The Journal of a Psychotherapist*. London: Jane Haynes.

Hill, M. (2004) *Diary of a Country Therapist*. Binghampton: Haworth Press.

Holzer, B.N. (1994) *A Walk Between Heaven and Earth, A Personal Journal on Writing and the Creative Process*. New York: Harmony Books.

Housman, A.E. (1994) 'Blue Remembered Hills'. In *Collected Poems of A.E. Housman*. Ware: Wordsworth Poetry Library (Original poem published 1896).

Hunt, C. (2000) *Therapeutic Dimensions of Autobiography in Creative Writing*. London: Jessica Kingsley Publishers.

James, W. (2007) *The Principles of Psychology*, Vol. 1. New York: Cosimo Classics (Original work published 1892).

Joyce, J. (2000) *Ulysses*. London: Penguin.

Jung, C.G. (1995) *Memories, Dreams and Reflections*. London: Fontana Press (Original work published 1962).

Lewis, G. (2007) *Sunbathing in the Rain: A Cheerful Book about Depression*. London: Jessica Kingsley Publishers.

Lively, P. (2005) *Making it Up*. London: Penguin Books.

Longo, P. (2006) *With Nothing Behind but Sky*. Santa Barbara: Artamo Press.

Michaels, A. (2000) 'The Hooded Hawk.' In A. Michaels *Poems*. London: Bloomsbury.

Milner, M. (1986) *An Experiment in Leisure*. London: Virago.

Morisette, P.J. (2001) *Self-supervision: A Primer for Counselors and Helping Professionals*. Hove: Brunner-Routledge.

Moskowitz, C. (1998) 'The self as source: creative writing generated from personal reflection.' In C. Hunt and F. Sampson (eds) *The Self on the Page: Theory and Practice of Creative Writing in Personal Development.* London: Jessica Kingsley Publishers.

New, J. (2005) *Drawing from Life: The Journal as Art.* New York: Princeton Architectural Press.

Pennebaker, J. (1990) *Opening Up, The Healing Power of Expressing Emotions.* New York: The Guilford Press.

Perry, S.K. (1999) *Writing in Flow.* Cincinnati: Writer's Digest Books.

Prochaska, J.O., Norcross, J.C. and Diclemente, C.C (1994) *Changing for Good: The Revolutionary Program That Explains the Six Stages of Change and Teaches You How to Free Yourself from Bad Habits.* New York: William Morrow.

Progoff, I. (1975) *At a Journal Workshop: Writing to Access the Power of the Unconscious and Evoke Creative Ability.* New York: Dialogue House Library.

Rainer, T. (1977) *The New Diary.* Los Angeles: Jeremy P. Tarcher.

Rubin, L. (1996) *The Transcendent Child.* New York: Basic Books.

Rush, C. (2005) *To Travel Hopefully: Journal of a Death not Foretold.* London: Profile Books.

Ryle, A. (2004) 'Writing by patients and therapists in cognitive analytic therapy.' In G. Bolton, S. Howlett, C. Lago and J. Wright (eds) *Writing Cures.* Hove: Brunner-Routledge.

Schneider, M. and Killick, J. (1998) *Writing for Self Discovery.* Shaftesbury: Element Books.

Shohet, R. (ed.) (2008) *Passionate Supervision.* London: Jessica Kingsley Publishers.

Silverstone, L. (2009) *Art Therapy Exercises.* London: Jessica Kingsley Publishers.

Smith, A. (2006) *The Accidental.* New York: Pantheon.

Snow E.R. (2000) *Personal Writings of Eliza Roxcy Snow.* Salt Lake City: University of Utah Press.

Styron, W. (2001) *Darkness Visible: A Memoir of Madness.* London: Vintage.

Thompson, K. (2004) 'Journal writing as a therapeutic tool.' In G. Bolton, S. Howlett, C. Lago and J. Wright (eds) *Writing Cures.* Hove: Brunner-Routledge.

Thompson, K. (2006) 'Dear Ray.........love Jean.' In G. Bolton, V. Field and K. Thompson (eds) *Writing Works.* London: Jessica Kingsley Publishers.

Thompson, K. and Wright, J.K. (2006) 'Coming out as writing therapists.' *Lapidus Quarterly* 2, 1, 17–20.

Truman, J. (1988) *Letter to my Husband. Notes about Mourning and Recovery.* London: Penguin Books.

Van Deurzen, E. (2008) *What is the Existential Approach?* Available at www.dilemmaconsultancy.org/the-existential-approach.html, accessed on 23 October 2009.

Van Deurzen, E. (2009) *Everyday Mysteries: Existential Dimensions of Psychotherapy.* London: Routledge.

Waugh, E. (1962) *Brideshead Revisited.* London: Penguin Books.

White, M. (2007) *Maps of Narrative Practice.* New York: W.W. Norton.

White, M. and Epston, D. (1990) *Narrative Means to Therapeutic Ends.* New York: W.W. Norton.

Wolton, R. (2006) 'Critic Tango: A workshop on the inner critic.' In G. Bolton, V. Field and K. Thompson (eds) *Writing Works*. London: Jessica Kingsley Publishers.

Woods, P. (1998) *Diary of a Grief.* York: The Ebor Press.

Woolf, V. (1994) *To the Lighthouse.* Ware: Wordsworth Classics.

Woolf, V. (1997) *A Moment's Liberty.* London: Pimlico.

Wright, J. (2009) 'Dialogical journal writing as "Self-therapy": "I matter".' *Counselling and Psychotherapy Research 9*, 4, 235–240.

Yalom, I. (2005) *The Theory and Practice of Group Psychotherapy.* New York: Basic Books.

Yalom I. (2008) *Staring at the Sun.* London: Piatkus.

Index

219